THE TWO WHEELS OF DHAMMA

AAR STUDIES IN RELIGION

Number Three

THE TWO WHEELS OF DHAMMA

Essays on the Theravada Tradition in India and Ceylon

by

GANANATH OBEYESEKERE
University of Ceylon

FRANK REYNOLDS
University of Chicago

BARDWELL L. SMITH, *Editor*
Carleton College

Chambersburg, Pennsylvania
American Academy of Religion
1972

Library of Congress Catalog Card Number: 70-188906

Copyright © American Academy of Religion

PRINTED IN THE UNITED STATES OF AMERICA
PRINTING DEPARTMENT, UNIVERSITY OF MONTANA, MISSOULA, MONTANA 59801

 55

Contents

Introduction

The present collection of essays deals with a number of interrelated themes which provide the volume with a cohesiveness that is splendidly accidental, though seemingly planned *ab ovo*. To be sure, manuscripts were solicited from persons with known research interests in the general area of Theravada Buddhism and the social order. For reasons of length primarily the volume was limited to five essays, though there were several others which might well have been selected. One decision which helped delimit the scope and provide a kind of focus was to include papers dealing only with historical Theravada in India and Ceylon and with contemporary developments within Sinhalese Buddhism. Even here, essays were chosen which dealt expressly with the social order.

Beyond these very general rubrics the aim of the editor was to assemble a number of essays which directly or indirectly paid attention to the complex interplay in Buddhism and Buddhist society between *ānācakka* and *dhammacakka*, between "temporality" and "spirituality," or between worldly power and the power of righteousness. The very difficulty of providing adequate glosses for these Pali terms is symptomatic of the problems of interpreting clearly the intriguing interplay between them which has been present throughout Theravada history, in Burma and Thailand in their own ways as in India and Ceylon.

Present discussions of analogous themes, whether within Asian contexts or those in the West, have not infrequently settled for certain terms which often beg more questions than they resolve. One thinks especially of terms such as "secular" and "sacred," or "this-worldly" and "other-worldly." Any series of terms is no more than an attempt to capture very complex phenomena; the ones used in these essays may prove no less unsatisfactory. They are, at any rate, as much an attempt to raise further questions about the realities observed as to express misgivings about other sorts of labels. It was felt, however, that the traditional dichotomies more frequently masked than revealed the relationships between "religion" and "society" which have historically been operative within the Theravada scene. Ultimately, there is the effort here to describe and assess the various ways in which Buddhist religious values, conceptions and activities have served to shape the so-called non-religious spheres of Buddhist societies. At first glance, even such a statement merely begs its own set of questions.

The very title given to this collection, *The Two Wheels of Dhamma*, is indicative of the attempt made to highlight the continuing tension in Theravada between the wheel of power (*ānācakka*) and the wheel of righteousness (*dhammacakka*). At its worst, the tension collapses either into a usurping of power by temporal authorities, normally by the state though sometimes even by elements within the Sangha, or into an indifference toward matters temporal through a misconceived notion of *Nibbāna*. At its best, however, the tension signifies a

1

sustained awareness of the necessary interrelationship (symbiosis, syzygy) of these two wheels — one which affirms the legitimacy, indeed necessity, of the political and social and economic well-being of persons in community, the other which points through mythology, symbolism, sacred writings, and human paradigms to dimensions of spirit without which existence remains endless suffering.

While the term "other-worldly" has important references within the Theravada tradition, it is not an appropriate designation of *Nibbāna*, which connotes release from suffering and the achieving of enlightenment, not escape from the affairs of worldly existence. The paradigm par excellence is, of course, the Buddha in whom the tension between compassionate involvement with those in suffering and freedom from attachment himself was maintained throughout. As the opening essay by Frank Reynolds states clearly, interpretations of Theravada which portray it in gnostic terms provide an unbalanced picture which ignores both the origin and the historical development of this tradition.

It is perhaps because Buddhism's soteriological mission is sometimes misconstrued in this fashion that release from suffering is viewed as escape from phenomenal existence, while in actuality it means triumph over attachment to (or craving after) matters either "temporal" or "spiritual". It is precisely this sort of release or freedom which is best able to maintain an appropriate tension between the two wheels, a tension which not only sees ambiguity within everything, the so-called good and the so-called evil, but which affirms the social order without regarding its ways or standards as normative. If soteriological images appear fanciful, "other-worldly" or remote from what men normally see or experience, it is not because enlightenment or salvation belongs to another world but because its dimensions require an integrity all men paradoxically resist yet inevitably seek.

The primal instance of ambiguity is the combined affirmation of political power with reservation about its capacity to become self-corrupting. Sovereignty, as exercised by the monarch or in other forms, is portrayed in the *Mahāvaṃsa* as "sweet food mixed with poison," not because power inevitably corrupts but because all men deal with the forces of *adhamma* (or chaos) within and in the power of a sovereign its dangers are understandably the greater. The first two essays especially deal at considerable length with various concepts (e.g., the *Cakkavatti*, the *Mahāsammata*, the *Mahāpurisa*, and the *Bodhisattva*) which by definition were attempts within the Buddhist tradition in its developing history in India and Ceylon to comprehend the interplay between temporal and spiritual forces in modes that preserved a sense of realism alongside a vision of harmonious order.

It was perceived from the beginning within Theravada that the achievement of a righteous order within and between men depended in no small way upon the maintaining of reasonable stability and justice within the social order. Even more important than the monarch's role as patron of the Sangha was his political function as the regulator of order within society, for without minimal stability the greater quest for *Nibbāna* was imperiled. Threats to the Sangha were inevitably of one piece with threats to the social fabric as a whole.

The model of Asoka looms larger with the passage of time, becoming archetypal not only of all rulers in relationship to the Sangha but of all men with respect to the exercise of temporal power and the reconciliation of the two wheels in personal and collective terms. As the image of Asoka gathered deeper significance in Sinhalese and Burmese interpretations, there was the concomitant portrayal of the Buddha in ways which fused the historic Gotama, in Reynolds' words, with various themes of "a pre-existing royal mythology." The alternate destinies put before the infant Siddhattha, as either Buddha-Teacher or Cakkavatti-King, come to be seen as inseparably related in his basic vocation as "world-conqueror," one whose enlightened compassion occasions the uniting of temporal and spiritual authority.

It is only in relationship to a vividly realistic awareness of man's capacity for evil and a persisting sensitivity to the threat of disorder that the Buddhist soteriological images retain their hold upon the imagination. The sensed interconnection between the interior life of each person, the quality of existence within a community, and the very condition of the cosmos itself affords spatial and temporal dimensions to both suffering and freedom which give them epic proportion. The Asokan odyssey from self-seeking power to benevolent authority becomes a repeated refrain of how power itself is not simply to be renounced but rather transformed. The dilemma which no man, certainly no monarch, can escape is seen to have been resolved by Asoka who stands apart as the embodiment of *ānācakka* in service to a higher righteousness, a foretaste of the eschatological conquest of suffering itself (*dhammavijaya*).

Into this framework which combines a vision of genuine harmony with the continued experiencing of distress and enmity is set the relationship between monarch and Sangha which is the prototype of the tension between the two wheels. If the bhikkhu community is sometimes romanticized as having a vocation higher than that of king and the laity in general, it is false to portray its members as immune from the same struggles encountered by other men. The chronicles of Ceylon are especially instructive here in their acknowledging of "lawless monks" and their stress upon *sāsana* reform. If the *bhikkhu-sangha* has its special vocation of pointing to the Dhamma and of seeking its rule with fewer distractions, it is not coextensive with the *sāvaka-sangha* which is an invisible community of the enlightened (lay and bhikkhu alike) whose qualities are beyond empirical validation yet whose catalytic power and effect are extraordinary.

Again, the prevailing self-image, sustained through centuries of experience with the dilemmas of power, emerges as graphically ambiguous. *Dhammadīpa*, the Island of the Law (Ceylon), is viewed as both the archetype of delusion and the paragon of enlightenment. It is clearly through forgetfulness of this reality that men are tempted to ignore the necessary tension between *ānācakka* which restrains society from falling prey to chaos and *dhammacakka* which not only checks temporal power but points beyond it to dimensions of power purged of self-seeking. Against this background also the contemporary struggles of Sinhalese Buddhism must be viewed.

The saga of Ceylon's relationship to foreign powers (to India through most of her history, including the present; to Western nations through four centuries of colonialism and beyond) provides important clues to her sense of self-esteem which over time has vacillated between an appropriate pride in the richness of her culture and continuing apprehension about its vulnerability. While not appearing for the first time in the mid-nineteenth century, it is clear that the contrast between what Ceylon had once been and what she had become began to emerge in powerful form about a hundred years ago. Though not yet adequately told, this story is a familiar one and includes such ingredients as the Buddhist-Christian debates, the stirrings of Buddhist modernism, the growth of Ceylonese nationalism and the reemergence of Sinhalese self-consciousness. Political and economic components are woven inevitably into the communalism of recent decades and into the immense ambivalence Sinhalese elements especially display toward Western culture. If the present problems within Ceylon stem to a considerable degree from the absence of a diversified economy, it is crucial that they be seen within the larger and more ancient question of self-identity.

The essay by Gananath Obeyesekere captures in a perceptive manner the ambivalence displayed by forms of contemporary Sinhalese Buddhism toward the organizational profile of modern society and the attempt by religious traditions to address themselves to urban and industrialized contexts. In many respects what is visible within Ceylon is in no sense absent elsewhere. The organizational and technological developments the world over confront all forms of traditional values and structures with painful dilemmas. The simple choices of either ignoring the modern world or of rejecting entirely the claims of tradition and history are, in the long run, seldom satisfactory. In-between remains the bewildering prospect of creating values, structures and goals out of claims and precedents from other cultures combined with renewed appropriation of forms intrinsic to one's past. While Ceylon's task resembles that found in all societies today, it is also true that there are ingredients here which are unique or in different form. And, in terms of Theravada Buddhism, there are forces present which have no historical precedent and which present opportunities that are inevitably ambiguous.

The most crucial of these is what Obeyesekere calls the "spatial shift" of Buddhist attention and activity away from the traditional monastic separation from society toward serious involvement in a number of social and political arenas. The ambivalence which accompanies this shift is forcefully expressed by monks and laymen alike, many of whom regard it as the downfall of the Sangha while others herald it as the re-creation of Buddhist influence upon affairs of state and communal life. Potentially both, its recent history has brought the exhilaration of new energy alongside communal violence, divisions within the Sangha and enormous confusion about what vocation is appropriate to laymen as well as bhikkhus.

In a certain sense, the spatial shift is without precedent, though the history of Theravada in Ceylon and India reveals constant interplay, as we have suggested, between the two wheels of Dhamma, an interplay which had been immobilized in recent centuries for a number of reasons. The new factor, which has no precedent, is the emergence into the middle class of an educated laity whose relationship to both the Sangha and the temporal power brings features which complicate still further the role Theravada will play in Ceylon or elsewhere. The tendencies toward a secularism which displaces any Buddhist claim upon the central issues of freedom, order or justice is only reinforced by tendencies within the *sāsana* toward narrow codes of ethics which preserve a kind of purity but at the expense of a sophisticated redefinition not only of how *ānācakka* and *dhammacakka* may be kept in tension but of how this tension may be supportive of the larger vision to which Theravada, as all Buddhism, points, a vision with sociological as well as soteriological implications. As Frank Reynolds has implied, this is a task which faces the *Ecclesia* in Christianity and the *Ummah* in Islam no less than the Buddhist *Saṅgha*. It is the task of perceiving the sacral reality within and beyond the institutional and value frameworks of the social order.

In the following essays Sanskrit and Pali terms, not proper nouns, are in italics the first time they are used, with appropriate diacritical marks. Thereafter, they are without diacritical marks and are not italicized.

BARDWELL L. SMITH
Carleton College

The Two Wheels of Dhamma:
A Study of Early Buddhism

FRANK REYNOLDS

SALVATION AND ORDER

Religions at various levels of human history have expressed a concern both for the attainment of personal salvation and for the establishment and maintenance of proper order in the world. Among many primitive peoples the close correspondence between the ideal which men envisioned and the actualities of the world in which they lived allowed the two concerns to remain largely undifferentiated. In situations such as those depicted by Stanner in his study of the Australian Murumbutu, and by Layard in his work on the Melanesian people of the island of Malakula, personal religious fulfillment or salvation—though differently experienced in each situation—was realized in and through activities which also served to preserve and celebrate the traditional order of life.[1] As Joseph Kitagawa has noted, men in such primitive contexts have tended to understand themselves as "a part of society which is in turn an integral part of nature and the cosmos."[2]

In the more urban and cosmopolitan contexts where the classical religious traditions have developed, the situation became considerably more complex. To a much greater degree than in the primitive societies there emerged individuals and movements which challenged the ultimate significance of the traditional sacred order and in many cases these individuals and movements went still further and called into question the meaning of this-worldly existence as such. Sages and prophets appeared who recognized a radically different and transcendent mode of reality and the capacity of men to break free from their natural and social condition in order to attain it. In some of the classical religions, especially those such as Judaism, Confucianism, and Shinto which were closely identified with the political and cultural traditions of a particular ethnic group, the new forms of other-worldly soteriology played only a limited role. On the other hand, in many of the mystery religions and in a number of gnostic sects the religious

---

[1] W. E. H. Stanner, *On Aboriginal Religion* (Oceania Monograph, No. 11; Sydney: University of Sydney, n.d.); John Willoughby Layard, *Stone Men of Malakula* (London: Chatto and Windus, 1942).

[2] Joseph M. Kitagawa, "Chaos, Order and Freedom in World Religions," in Paul Kuntz, ed., *The Concept of Order* (Seattle: University of Washington, 1967), p. 278. The same point has been made by Robert Bellah in his article "On Religious Evolution," in William A. Lessa and Evon Z. Vogt, eds., *Reader in Comparative Religion* (2d ed.; New York: Harper and Row, 1965).

ideal came to be focused on a personal soteriological quest and the concern for order in this-worldly existence was either ignored or radically rejected. Finally, however, in several of the more inclusive traditions such as Islam, Christianity, and Hinduism, there developed a creative tension and various syntheses between other-worldly and less radical soteriologies on the one hand, and between personal soteriological goals and the concern for proper ordering of this-worldly life on the other.[3]

Given this way of viewing the classical religions, early Buddhism presents something of a puzzle. From simply reading the discussions of many Buddhologists one could easily be tempted to understand the tradition as one in which the quest for personal salvation from the suffering of this-worldly life led to the neglect or radical rejection of the concern for proper order within it—that is to say, one would be tempted to classify early Buddhism in the same category with the mystery religions and gnostic sects. And, as a matter of fact, efforts have been made to argue for just this kind of interpretation. A number of nineteenth- and early twentieth-century scholars sought to interpret Buddhism within the context of gnosticism; and as late as 1953 Paul Levy devoted his Jordan lectures to an interpretation of Buddhism as a mystery religion.[4] However, in spite of the numerous parallels which clearly do exist between early Buddhism and certain gnostic and mystery traditions, a wholistic view of early Buddhism reveals the presence of many important elements which cannot be encompassed within this kind of understanding. Like early Christianity, which in the not too distant past was also subjected to narrow and falsifying interpretations along strictly gnostic or mystery cult lines, early Buddhism incorporated strands of other-worldly soteriology, an interest in more immediately accessible soteriological goals, and a concern for the establishment and maintenance of proper order in the world.

And what is particularly important for our purposes, each of these emphases made a crucial impact on the way in which the early Buddhists related their tradition to the symbolism and institutions of sacral kingship.

THE HISTORICAL CONTEXT

During the middle centuries of the first millenium B. C. there existed a broad area extending across southern Eurasia from Greece in the West to the Huang Ho and Yangtze in the Far East within which important and generally parallel economic, political, and religious transformations were taking place. It was a time in which civilizations which had long been established in widely separated centers were expanding, developing, and coming into increasing contact. In an attempt

[3] For a discussion of these tensions and interactions, see *From Max Weber: Essays in Sociology*, trans., ed., and with an Introduction by H. H. Gerth and C. Wright Mills (Oxford: Oxford University, 1958), pp. 267-362.

[4] Paul Levy, *Buddhism: A "Mystery" Religion?* Jordan Lectures, 1953 (London: Athlone, 1957). For a discussion of the gnostic interpretations, see Guy Richard Welbon, *The Buddhist Nirvāna and Its Western Interpreters* (Chicago: University of Chicago Press, 1968), pp. 4-10.

to characterize this situation Joseph Campbell has suggested the presence of what he calls a "mythogenic zone," "a limited yet sufficiently broad area of the earth's surface, relatively uniform in character, where a large population of closely related individuals (here those inhabiting the broad domain of late early Iron Age societies) became affected simultaneously by roughly comparable imprints (those of an emergent urban domesticity), and where, consequently, psychological 'seizures' of like kind were everywhere impending and, in fact, became precipitated in a context of ritualized procedure and myth."[5] Karl Jaspers and Lewis Mumford have used the term "axial breakthrough" to refer to the transformation which took place and have identified some of the major cross-cultural characteristics. They have pointed out that it involved the emergence of a new consciousness of the individual and the possibilities for personal salvation as well as a closely correlated emphasis on less parochial, more universal orientations and values; they have pointed to the appearance of a more radical sense of ontological transcendence and a corresponding devaluation of this-worldly, phenomenal existence; and they have noted the formation of new patterns of institutional life, both specifically religious and more political, which expressed and disseminated these new discoveries.[6] In the intellectual and religious spheres these new tendencies were clearly manifested in the appearance of a philosophic tradition and the Academy as well as the mystery cults in Greece, of the prophets and prophetic schools in the ancient Near East, of Confucian thought and the classic *jen* tradition in China, of the Upanishadic sages and the communities of forest dwellers in India, and of founded religions such as Zoroastrianism, Jainism, and Buddhism. In the more political sphere many of the same tendencies were reflected in the new cosmopolitan empires such as those associated with Alexander in the Hellenistic world, with the Ch'in and Han dynasties in China, with Darius and Cyrus in Persia, and with the Mauryas in India.

Within this broad historical context each region had a unique heritage and conditions which led to a development which had its own very specific characteristics. For example, in northeastern India—the area in which Buddhism emerged and therefore the one which particularly interests us—the new tendencies appeared in the midst of a process of interaction between Aryan and pre-Aryan traditions which had long been at the core of ancient Indian history.[7] At this particular time (*ca.* eighth-fifth centuries B.C.) the Aryanized Brahmanic traditions which had been shaped and become firmly established in northwestern and north central India were being imported and adapted by the indigenous

    [5] Joseph Campbell, *The Masks of God: Oriental Mythology* (New York: Viking Press, 1962), pp. 251-252.

    [6] Karl Jaspers, *The Origin and Goal of History*, trans. by Michael Bullock (New Haven: Yale University Press, 1965); Lewis Mumford, *The Transformations of Man* (New York: Harper, 1956).

    [7] For a discussion of the state of our knowledge concerning the Aryan invaders and the nature of their interaction with the indigenous population, see Louis Renou, *Religions of Ancient India* (London: Athlone Press, 1953), pp. 1-45.

populations farther to the east.[8] In the northeastern area, categories of religious reflection such as *Rta-Dharma*, *karma*, and *ātman* which had already made their appearance and accumulated a web of specifically Vedic-Brahmanic meanings were taken over and given new evaluations and significance. Types of religious practice, notably yogic techniques and various forms of asceticism which had already become integrated into the Brahmanic tradition reappeared in this new context in close association with semi- or non-Brahmanic teachings, for example those of Samkhya and the Ajivakas. And, at the level of religious leadership and community, the groups of wandering mendicants which had made their appearance at the Upanishadic level of the Vedic-Brahmanic tradition became much more numerous and influential as this new cultural situation developed farther to the east.[9] Significantly, it was among the wandering mendicant groups in the eastern regions that the radically new religious orientations such as Jainism and Buddhism made their appearance.

The religious developments in northeastern India during this period were also closely bound up with a very rapid disintegration in the traditional tribal patterns of life. As the Indian Marxist historian D. D. Kosambi has emphasized in a number of his works, the introduction of iron into India in the eighth century B.C. and its subsequent use in the development of more effective methods of forest clearing led to an increase in the intensity of agricultural cultivation, particularly in the Ganges Valley.[10] With the growing agricultural base and the valuable mineral deposits which were discovered, this region soon became very much involved in the system of trade and commerce which was developing across all of northern India and even beyond. Urban centers were established and soon became the focal points around which the life of the area was organized. In this situation a significant number of people, having been cut off from the old sources of order and meaning, and not being able to discern viable alternatives, began to experience a sense of lostness and despair. Others, particularly the merchants and city dwellers, were open to more relevant ways of expressing their religious concerns and were quite ready to support those engaged in new forms of religious and intellectual endeavor. In his book, *Kingship and Community in Early India*, Charles Drekmeier, a sociologist who is seeking to carry on in the tradition of Max Weber, speaks of this breakdown of the long established archaic patterns as a "tribal trauma."[11] And he goes on to point out that early Buddhism and the

---

[8] For a discussion of the situation in northeastern India, see Damodar D. Kosambi, *An Introduction to the Study of Indian History* (Bombay: Popular Book Depot, 1956).

[9] Though there are numerous theories concerning the origin of the wandering mendicant community, Sukumar Dutt's contention that it emerged out of the encounter of the Brahmanical forms developed in northwestern India and the indigenous culture of the northeast is most convincing. See his discussion in *Early Buddhist Monachism* (London: Asia Publishing House, 1960).

[10] For example, see Kosambi, *Indian History*, *passim*.

[11] Charles Drekmeier, *Kingship and Community in Early India* (Palo Alto: Stanford University Press, 1962), p. 63.

development of the Magdhan state, which culminated in the rule of the Mauryas and the reign of Asoka, may appropriately be interpreted as two distinct but converging responses to this highly threatening but also challenging situation.[12]

THE FOUNDER

The appearance of charismatic personalities at times of profound human crisis is a phenomenon which can be documented at all levels of human history. The more specific appearance of religious founders is, however, a much rarer occurrence. In fact, with the perhaps questionable exceptions of Moses and Zoroaster, the Buddha and his slightly older contemporary Mahavira (sometimes considered to be the founder of the Jains) are the first about whom we have any knowledge.[13]

As in the case of all the classical religious founders, the relationship between the actual historical experience and events of the Buddha's lifetime and the way in which these experiences were remembered and recorded by his followers is very complex and difficult to specify precisely.[14] Some scholars such as Ananda Coomaraswamy have maintained that the mythic elements were prior and of central importance, and have considered the historical Gotama Buddha to be at most a reformer with whom these mythic elements happened to become associated.[15] Others, especially the early philologists of the Pali school, have recognized the historical Buddha as a great and almost totally original genius whose personality and insights were very soon overlaid and vulgarized by the popular mythology and superstitions of the day.[16] However, it is very hard to reconcile either of these extreme positions with what historians of religions have discovered in their cross-cultural studies of religious founders, and with the texts which provide our primary source material.

As in the case of most other founders, the late historical date and confessional nature of the sources which we possess make any attempt to reconstruct a modern style biography of the Buddha quite impossible.[17] Nevertheless, it is clear that

---

[12] Drekmeier's interpretation (*ibid.*) places a strong emphasis on the distinction (Buddhism is, for him, primarily a psychological response), whereas our emphasis will be on the convergence.

[13] The close connection between the new religious insights associated with the so-called "axial age," especially the new sense of individuality, and the appearance of prophets and sages who were recognized as the founders of new religious communities, should not be overlooked.

[14] For general discussions of religious founders from the perspective of the history of religions, see Joachim Wach, *Sociology of Religion* (Chicago: University of Chicago Press, 1944), and G. Van der Leeuw, *Religion in Essence and Manifestation*, II, pp. 650-654.

[15] Ananda Coomaraswamy, *Hinduism and Buddhism* (New York: Philosophical Library, n.d.), pp. 46-47.

[16] For a discussion of such interpretations, see Edward Conze, *Thirty Years of Buddhist Studies: Selected Essays* (Columbia, S.C.: University of South Carolina Press, 1968), pp. 1-13.

[17] For the most responsible attempts to reconstruct the Buddha's life, see Edward Joseph

there was an historical founder of the Buddhist community and most scholars now agree that he was one of a number of mendicant Sramanas (Holy Men) who were teaching in the cities and villages of northeastern India during the latter part of the sixth century B.C. and the early part of the fifth.[18] Moreover, despite their diversity on many points of detail, the texts show that he was a charismatic personality in the classic Weberian sense, that he probably originated and certainly propounded a distinctive gospel which promised salvation to those with the ability and willingness to pursue it, and that he gathered around him a diversified group of disciples including wandering mendicants and nuns, as well as men and women who continued to live the life of householders.[19]

It is equally evident that in their efforts to express the deeply religious meaning which they had discovered in and through the Buddha's personality and activities, and in their attempts to preserve the immediacy of this meaning for themselves and others, his followers made extensive use of myths, symbols, and cultic action. During the lifetime of the Buddha himself his disciples began the process of remembering and reporting his activities, a process which finally reached its culmination in the rich and colorful sacred biographies which have become a basic element in the structure of the later traditions. And there are strong textual indications that even during his lifetime the tendency to venerate the Buddha's person began to make its appearance, and that it soon developed into a popular and highly adaptable devotional cult which became a hallmark of the tradition in every area where it was established.

Though the process and timing involved in the development of the sacred biography of the Buddha is still a matter of debate, considerable progress has been made through the use of text-critical methods. For example, Étienne La-Motte has reconstructed what he considers to be five identifiable stages of its evolution within the literature.[20] In the first two stages, which he identifies with the biographical fragments imbedded within the various canonical Suttas and Vinayas, he finds all of the major motifs which are present in the classical versions of the Buddha's life.[21] These motifs, he maintains, were all clearly estab-

Thomas, *The Life of Buddha as Legend and History* (London: K. Paul, Trench, Trubner & Co., Ltd.; New York: A. A. Knopf, 1927); and André Bareau, *Recherches sur la Biographie du Buddha dans les Sutrapitaka et les Vinayapitaka anciens: de la Quête de l'Éveil à la conversion de Saraputra et de Maudgalyāyanal* (Paris: École Française d'Extrême-Orient, 1963).

[18] For a review of the various theories of the dating of the Buddha's life, see Madan Mohan Singh, "The Date of Buddha-Nirvana," *Journal of Indian History*, XXXIX, No. 3 (December, 1961), pp. 359-363.

[19] For one of Weber's many discussions of charisma and charismatic authority, see Gerth and Mills, *From Max Weber*, pp. 245-252.

[20] Étienne LaMotte, *Histoire du Bouddhisme indien* (Louvain: Publications Universitaires, 1958), pp. 713-751. See also his "La legende du Bouddha," *Revue de l'Histoire des Religions*, CXXXIV (1947-1948), pp. 37-41.

[21] Erich Frauwallner, in *The Earliest Vinaya and the Beginnings of Buddhist Literature* (Serie Orientale Roma, No. 8; Rome: Instituto Italiano per il Medio ed Estremo Oriente,

lished in the Magadhan period, that is to say before the end of the fourth century B.C. The third stage he associates with the independent but incomplete biographies such as the *Lalitavistara* and the *Mahāvastu* which he dates near the beginning of the Christian era; and the fourth is represented by the full scale independent biographies such as the one presently found in the Vinaya of the Mulasarvastivadins and the *Buddhacaritas* of Samgharaksa and Asvagosha, all of which, according to his reckoning, made their appearance around 200 A.D. At these third and fourth levels the events of the Buddha's career are presented in a considerably more dramatic form, and there is a much greater emphasis on miraculous elements. Finally, LaMotte associates the fifth stage of the development with the Pali compilations made during the fifth century A.D., compilations in which many of the elements which had appeared in later Sanskrit tradition were taken over by the Theravadins and rendered in accordance with their own more restrained style of presentation.[22] In this context, it is significant to note that the major text of this genre constitutes the introduction to the great Pali commentary on the *Jātaka* tales, a commentary which thus brings together the traditions which had developed concerning the Buddha's final life with the equally important traditions concerning the many earlier lives through which the Bodhisatta had prepared himself for his ultimate enlightenment and mission.

At the same time the work of other scholars has thrown considerable light on the parallel development of Buddha symbols and the devotional cult which centered around them.[23] Such works have confirmed the presence and importance of relics associated with the Founder within at least 50 years of his death and have revealed the importance of the closely correlated practice of constructing and venerating stupas dedicated to him. And they have highlighted the early tradition of representing the Buddha only in aniconic modes (for example, a footprint, a throne, a Bodhi tree, or a stupa), the transition through which certain key symbols of his presence gradually took on a more explicitly cosmological significance, and the emergence, near the beginning of the Christian era, of iconic representations and the cult of images.[24]

In this process through which the Buddhist community expressed and enriched the meaning which it perceived in the life of its Founder many new elements were introduced. However, among these none were more important

1956), has reconstructed a complete biography which he believes was composed approximately 100 years after the Buddha's death. However, his argument, though it has been accepted by several scholars including Edward Conze (*Buddhist Studies*, p. 8) is not fully convincing. For a refutation, see LaMotte, *Bouddhisme indien*, pp. 195-197.

[22] It should be emphasized that this post-canonical biography is the first complete biography of the Buddha to appear within the Pali tradition.

[23] Perhaps the most important single study is still Paul Mus, *Barabadur: Esquisse d'une histoire du bouddhisme fondée sur la critique archeologique des textes* (Paris: Paul Geuthner, 1935).

[24] As Mus (*ibid.*) has made very clear, the movement from aniconic to iconic forms of representation indicates a change from one religious mode to another and not, as some have assumed, a change from an original nihilistic philosophy toward popular superstition.

than the mythical motifs and symbols associated with sacred kings and specifically with the pre-Buddhist figure of the *Cakkavatti* (the Wheel-Turning Universal Monarch). The Sutra tradition contains several passages which rather soberly recount the purity of Gautama's genealogy and a number of the events in his career between his decision to leave the household life and the first sermon which he preached after attaining Enlightenment and Buddhahood. But in addition the Sutta collection includes two other biographical segments which are especially interesting for our purposes. One of these is the *Mahāvadana Sutta* which describes the career of a previous Buddha named Vipasyin, a career which is presented as archetypal for all the Buddhas who succeeded him, including Gotama.[25] This description begins with the future Buddha's descent from the Tusita heaven and his miraculous birth, and continues through his Enlightenment and first sermon to the point in his career when he gives the rules of the Order to his mendicant followers; and in the course of the narration it presents a variety of mythic motifs which relate the Buddha's career directly to the career of the Cakkavatti. For example, immediately after his birth the future Buddha is examined by the wise men of his father's court and is found to possess the 32 bodily marks which distinguish a *Mahāpurisa*, a Great Man who is destined to choose either the vocation of a Buddha-Teacher or the vocation of a Cakkavatti-King. Or, to cite another example which adds a new dimension since it occurs after the Enlightenment, the Buddha's first sermon is described as his setting in motion the wheel of *Dhamma*, an act which is the prerogative par excellence of the Cakkavatti.

The other mythically oriented biographical material found at this level of the canonical literature is contained in the justly famous and extensively studied *Mahāparinibbāna Sutta*, a text which describes the last days and immediate aftermath of the Buddha's earthly career. [26] Again in this text, we find the Buddha depicted as a Mahapurisa possessing the 32 bodily marks, but here new elements are included as well.[27] For example, in the midst of the narration the Buddha indicates that he has chosen the place for his earthly demise on the basis of the fact that in seven of his earlier lives he had been a Cakkavatti whose capital had been located at that particular spot. Much more important, the text explicitly states that as a Buddha he merits and receives the same elaborate funerary rites which are otherwise performed only for a Cakkavatti. Moreover, like a Cakka-

[25] *The Dialogues of the Buddha II*, trans. by T. W. and C. A. F. Rhys Davids, Vol. III of *The Sacred Books of the Buddhists*, ed. by T. W. Rhys Davids (14 vols.; London: Oxford University Press, 1895-1951), pp. 4-41. (*Dīgha Nikāya* II, xiv, 1-33). Following this, reference to this series will be cited as *Sacred Books*.

[26] *The Dialogues of the Buddha II*, Vol. III of *The Sacred Books*, pp. 78-191 (*Dīgha Nikāya II*, xvi).

[27] For a recent discussion of the subject, see André Bareau, "The Superhuman Personality of Buddha and Its Symbolism in the Mahaparinirvanasutra of the Dharmagupta," in *Myths and Symbols: Studies in Honor of Mircea Eliade*, ed. by Joseph M. Kitagawa and Charles H. Long, with the collaboration of Jerald C. Brauer and Marshall G. S. Hodgson (Chicago and London: University of Chicago Press, 1969), pp. 9-22.

vatti (and lesser Buddhas and arhats), a funerary mound or stupa is raised over
his ashes and like a Cakkavatti (and lesser Buddhas and arhats), he merits and
receives offerings of perfumes, flowers, banners, parasols, and music.

In the later strata of biographical materials and in the growing cultic life of
the community, the tendency to incorporate royal, Cakkavatti elements is carried
still further. In the biographical segments of the Vinaya and in independent texts
such as the *Mahāvastu*, the *Buddhacaritas*, and the Pali *Nidānakatha*, these and
other cycles (for example, those dealing with the Buddha's genealogy, his birth,
his childhood, his great renunciation, his Enlightenment, his first sermon, certain
key events in his ministry, and his death) are woven together into an increasingly
more continuous and unified narrative in which the historical life of the Founder
and the royal mythology and symbolism are thoroughly fused. In this connection
it is interesting to note that in the Jataka tales (stories of the previous lives of
the Buddha), which became associated with the full sacred biography in the Pali
tradition, the future Buddha perfects both the virtues of kingship and the virtues
of renunciation, thus preparing the way for his attainment of the highest form of
Buddhahood in which the two strands receive their final synthesis and fulfillment.[28] On the cultic side the Founder came to be represented most commonly
and effectively through symbols closely identified with the Cakkavatti and to be
venerated in the context of rituals intimately bound up with sacral kingship. Certainly by the Asokan period the stupa and the stupa ceremonials such as those
referred to in the *Mahāparinibbāna Sutta* had assumed a place alongside the recitation of the Buddha's teaching as the dominant form of Buddhist cultic expression.[29] Moreover, when anthropomorphic Buddha images began to appear, the
tradition concerning the 32 marks played a central role in the iconography; and
when the cult had become more fully developed the royal symbolism was carried
so far that the practice of actually crowning images came into being, at least in
certain circles.[30]

The development of a sacred biography of the Founder incorporating the
major themes of a preexisting royal mythology and the closely correlated development of a cult centered around symbols and ceremonials shared with the royal
tradition are aspects of early Buddhism which have often been ignored or underestimated by those who have attempted to describe and interpret it. It is only by
taking them seriously into account, however, that one can hope to understand

---

[28] David Pierce, "The Middle Way Ethic of the *Jataka* Tales" (Unpublished paper
presented to the Buddhism Seminar, Carleton College, Northfield, Minnesota, August,
1968).

[29] Though less studied and less accessible, the importance of the cult should not be
underestimated. It may well be that Paul Mus is correct when he maintains that the cultic
development provided much of the impetus for the developments in the areas of mythology
and doctrine. See his *Barabadur*.

[30] Paul Mus, "Le Buddha paré: Son origine indienne: Cakyamuni dans le mahayanisme
moyen," *Bulletin de l'École Française Extrême Orient* (hereafter *BEFEO*), XXVIII (1928),
pp. 153-278.

not only the full range and richness of the early tradition itself, but also the close relationship between Buddhism and the institutions of sacral kingship which were to emerge in subsequent centuries.

DHAMMA AND KINGSHIP

The classical religious founders differ from other types of charismatic leaders in that their charismatic powers are intimately bound up with the discovery and proclamation of a distinctively new experience of religious reality. In the case of Jesus the experience and proclamation of the imminent coming of the Kingdom of God was the key element. In the case of Mohammed it was the experience and proclamation of a new and final Revelation from Allah which was crucial. In the case of the Buddha, on the other hand, it was his realization and proclamation of the Dhamma which enabled him to attract and maintain the loyalty of a large number of very diversified followers.[31]

In the earliest Buddhist traditions which are accessible to us Dhamma refers, first and foremost, to the sacred reality which the Buddha had discovered at the point of his Enlightenment. In this context it is recognized both as the Law which regulates and governs the totality of existence and, at the same time, as the Truth which enables men to break free from the limitations which existence imposes. Dhamma, in other words, was taken to be the source both of order in the world and salvation from it.[32]

Also at this very ancient level of the tradition, the Dhamma refers to the preaching through which the Buddha sought to convey the content, meaning, and benefits of his discovery. Since the Buddha's experience and therefore his insight into Dhamma was recognized as qualitatively superior to that which was accessible even to his most accomplished disciples, his utterances on matters of belief and practice were generally accepted by the community as authoritative and final. In this situation the correlation between the Dhamma understood as the ultimate Law and Truth and the Dhamma constituted by the teachings which were accepted as authentically his became very close indeed.

Although it is impossible to determine which, if any, of the specific passages recorded in the scriptures represent accurately remembered elements of the Bud-

---

[31] As in most parallel religious situations, the Buddha's discovery is recognized both as a new breakthrough and as the recovery of an ancient (or original) truth. For a discussion which emphasizes the latter aspect, see the chapter on "Yoga Techniques in Buddhism," in Mircea Eliade, *Yoga: Immortality and Freedom*, trans. by Willard R. Trask (Bollingen Series, Vol. LVI; New York: Pantheon Books, 1958).

[32] The interpretive literature on the early Buddhist Dhamma is vast. Its richness and subtlety are perhaps best conveyed in the intensive philological analysis of the meanings which the term itself has carried within the context of the Pali canon in Wilhelm Geiger and Magdalene Geiger, *Pali Dhamma: Vornehmlich in der kanonischen Literatur* (München: Verlag der Bayerischen Akademie der Wissenschaften, 1920). See also Edward Conze's recent essay, "Dharma as a Spiritual, Social, and Cosmic Force," in Kuntz, *Order*, pp. 239-252.

dha's own teaching, the overwhelming impression conveyed by the older strata of texts is that at this level of the tradition the Dhamma was understood and expounded primarily as a gospel through which men's suffering and sense of meaninglessness could be overcome. The Dhamma appears as a message being proclaimed "for the welfare of the many" and one which is always presented in accordance with the capacities, temperament, and needs of the particular individual or group being addressed.[33] As a message its basic intent does not seem to have been to present a doctrinal or philosophical system as such, but rather to convert the hearers to a radically new mode of life, to lead people, in other words, to enter into the Path through which salvation could actually be experienced. As Sukumar Dutt has pointed out in the introduction to his excellent book, *Buddhist Monks and Monasteries in India*, it was just this dynamic, missionary character of the early Buddhist preaching which distinguished it from the teachings of most of the contemporary Sramanas and sects, and accounted for its success.[34]

In the course of the centuries which followed, the Buddhist community sought to transmit the Dhamma which the Founder had discovered and preached; and in the process of creative transmission the original message was both codified and vastly enriched. On the one side, the preaching was organized into standard forms and its contents were reflected upon and gradually systematized into doctrinal and dogmatic positions. On the other hand, as the community expanded and confronted different problems and situations, new insights and formulations were developed and those which were considered to be true and appropriate were given the status of Buddha teachings and thus incorporated into the Dhamma. By the beginning of the Christian era this dual process of continuing systematization and enrichment had produced several versions of a canonical Dhamma which included a large collection of Suttas, a second large collection of materials dealing with the mendicant order and its discipline (the Vinaya), and a third collection of comparatively late doctrinal summaries known as the Abhidhamma or Higher Dhamma. Finally, a commentarial tradition became firmly established, and by the fifth century A.D. scholastic works such as Buddhagosha's *Path of Purification* in the Pali tradition, and Vasubandhu's *Abhidharmakośa* in the Sanskrit Sarvastivadin tradition, had become recognized as authoritative expressions of the Dhamma while other works which were filled with a great variety of legendary and popular materials (for example, the *Jātaka* and *Dhammapada* commentaries) had achieved a semi-canonical status and had assumed a vital role in the propagation of the faith.

As the early community gradually developed and extended its formulations

---

[33] The late Buddhist sources themselves distinguish between the doctrinally precise teachings of the Buddha (the nitartha sutras) and those specifically adapted to the condition of the hearers (the neyartha sutras); see, for example, *Abhidharmakosa de Vasubandhu*, tr. and ann. by L. de La Vallié Poussin (6 Vols., Paris: Paul Geuthner, 1923-1931), Vol. 5 (Chapters 7-9), p. 246ff.

[34] Sukumar Dutt, *Buddhist Monks and Monasteries in India: Their History and Their Contribution to Indian Culture* (New York: Humanities Press, 1962), pp. 19-34.

of the Dhamma, a number of royal symbols and traditions were incorporated and adapted to the new ethos. On the one hand, in their efforts to express the meaning of the Dhamma, as in their attempts to convey the meaning of the person of the Founder, the early Buddhists turned to the symbolism and images of sovereignty. For example, in the *Anguttara Nikāya* the Dhamma is referred to as the "ruler of rulers"[35] and again in the *Dīgha Nikāya* it is referred to as the "highest in the world," a description strongly suggesting the dimension of transcendence and sovereignty.[36] On the other side, as the community broadened its range of interests and its social involvement increased, the sociological and political aspects of the Dhamma were more explicitly formulated and integrated into the tradition.

In the canonical tradition there are some indications that the Buddha himself may have favored the older, tribal forms of republican polity which, during the time of his ministry, were operative both in the community from which he had himself come (the clan of Sakyans situated in what is now southern Nepal) and in some of the other groups such as the Vajjians who were still competing for power in northeastern India.[37] However, despite the polemic of some modern Buddhists who present their Founder as "the first great Democrat," there is no evidence that the Buddha recognized any basic conflict between the Dhamma and the monarchical forms of rule which were established in Magadha and Kosala where he did most of his preaching. On the contrary, there is considerable evidence to suggest that he and the early community sought royal favor and sympathy even to the extent of adapating the code of discipline in accordance with the wishes of important rulers.[38]

Within early Buddhism as a whole there was a basic acceptance of kingship as the normal and appropriate mode of government. To be sure, there is a strand within the tradition in which all the ordinary modes and institutions of this-worldly life are either ignored or rejected as religiously meaningless. And there is also a realistic appraisal of the dangers and abuses of royal power, a realism which is especially vivid at the more popular levels of the tradition. However, in spite of the importance of these elements, many recent scholars have recognized that among the early Buddhists there was a general acceptance of the necessity

[35] *The Book of the Gradual Sayings III*, trans. by E. M. Hare, Vol. XXV of the Translation Series of the Pali Text Society, ed. by C. A. F. Rhys Davids (27 vols.; London: Oxford University Press, 1913-36), p. 115. (Anguttara Nikāya III, cxxxii). This series will be cited as *Trans. Series.*

[36] *The Dialogues of the Buddha III.* Vol. IV of *Sacred Books*, pp. 90-92. (Dīgha Nikāya III, xxvii, 23-26).

[37] For a discussion of this issue and of the broader problem of the political orientation in early Buddhism, see Richard Gard, "Buddhism and Political Authority," in Harold W. Lasswell and Harlan F. Cleveland, eds., *The Ethic of Power: The Interplay of Religion, Philosophy and Politics* (Conference on Science, Philosophy, Religion in Relation to the Democratic Way of Life, No. 16; New York: Harper, 1962).

[38] *The Book of Discipline IV.* Vol. XIV of *Sacred Books*, p. 92. (Vinaya Pitaka IV. Mahāvagga I, 39, 1-4).

for maintaining at least minimum standards of order in society, and a related acceptance of the fact that kingship, in spite of the dangers which it involved, was an indispensable institution.[39] Moreover, there was a strong interest in articulating the implications of Dhamma for the ideals and institutions of kingship.

The canon and the commentaries are quite consistent concerning the basic responsibilities of the king and the ideal which he should seek to actualize. In practically all of the relevant passages it is either explicitly stated or implied that the ruler's primary task is the maintenance of order and justice in society and that the ideal is rule in accordance with the Dhamma. As one classic text states, the king must rely "just on Dhamma, honour Dhamma, esteem Dhamma as his standard and Mandate, and set Dhamma as the watch and bar and ward for folk within his realm."[40] When the passages are viewed more closely, however, it is clear that in the various segments of the literature there are important differences in interpretation and emphasis.

Perhaps the most restrained and certainly the most discussed of the positive interpretations of the nature and function of royal authority appears in the *Aggañña Sutta.*[41] In this text the process through which the world comes into being at the beginning of each cosmic cycle is described (in accordance with Buddhist principles the problem of absolute beginnings is not raised) and in this context the origin and raison d' être of kingship are portrayed. According to the myth, the process of devolution begins with the still existing, highly exalted and formless Brahma-beings who, because of their desire, "eat" more substantial food and thus descend to a lesser state; and it continues when the desire of these lesser beings leads to the consumption of still more material substance and the consequent appearance of successively lower cosmic levels and their inhabitants, until finally the world of men is brought into being. In this world, too, the devolution continues in a series of stages in which virtue declines and life becomes increasingly more difficult and troubled. When men begin to look down upon those whose appearance is inferior to their own, the rice plant which had grown of itself disappears and it becomes necessary to cultivate the land. Soon, as men seek to accumulate more rice than is required for their immediate needs, the rice fields are parcelled out among them, thus bringing private property into being and with it theft and lying, violence and punishment. In this situation, confronted with the necessity to maintain order, men gathered together and selected the one among them who was the most kind-hearted and authoritative to censure, to put down and to command, to drive away, to remove, commit and take away. They bestowed on him the title of *Mahāsammata* (the Great Elect), *Ksattiya*

---

[39] One of the better discussions is found in Balkrishna Gokhale, "Early Buddhist Kingship," *Journal of Asian Studies,* XXVI, No. 1 (November, 1966), pp. 15-22.

[40] *The Book of the Gradual Sayings III.* Vol. XXV of *Trans. Series,* p. 115. (Anguttara Nikāya III, cxxxii).

[41] *The Dialogues of the Buddha III.* Vol. IV of *Sacred Books,* p. 77. (Dīgha Nikāya III, xxvii).

(Lord of the Fields), and *Rājā* (because he agreed to protect the people with Dhamma) and committed themselves to provide one sixth of their rice crop as compensation for his protection and guidance.

This passage has attracted the interest of a number of historians and social scientists, primarily because it presents the first expression in the Indian literature of what they refer to as a social contract theory of the state and kingship, a theory which, as several of the interpreters have noted, is dependent on the new sense of the individual which was being nurtured in Buddhism and the other new soteriological religions.[42] It should be emphasized, however, that this particular Buddhist conception differs from the western and modern theories with which it has often been compared, for example that of Locke, in that it is placed within an explicitly religious context and expressed in characteristically religious forms.[43] The entire process of cosmic devolution which includes the decline of virtue and the agreement to establish a sovereign authority is regulated by the Sacred Law—the Dhamma—and is presented in vividly mythic terms. Moreover, the rule which is established through the consensus of the people is rule in accordance with the Dhamma or, to put it another way, a rule which actualizes as much of the Dhamma as is possible given the fallen state of humanity.

It is also worth noting that the special interests of the interpreters (including in this case both western scholars and modern Buddhist social theorists) have led to a somewhat one-sided emphasis on the principle of election enunciated in the text. To be sure, election is clearly set forth as the means through which the ruler is set in office. However, it is equally important to note that he received the approbation of the people because of his personal charisma and that it is this charismatic aspect which has been taken up and magnified in the commentaries and other later literature. For example, by the time of Buddhagosha the Mahasammata was considered to have been a Bodhisatta and in certain medieval traditions he came to be identified as the particular Bodhisatta who later attained Enlightenment as Gotama.[44]

A second major early Buddhist orientation toward kingship, also imbedded in a highly mythic context, focused around the figure of the Cakkavatti. Although there is a specific *Cakkavatti Sutta* in the *Dīgha Nikāya* which provides a starting point for understanding the conceptions which were associated with this figure, relevant references and allusions appear in many passages throughout the canon

---

[42] For a discussion of this development, see the appendix on "The Sociology of Early Buddhist Ethics," in Vishwanath Prasad Varma, *Studies in Hindu Political Thought and Its Metaphysical Foundations* (2nd ed., rev. and enl.; Delhi, Varanasi, and Patna: Motilal Barnasidas, 1959).

[43] The religious element in the Buddhist perspective is also missed in the otherwise excellent discussion by Louis Dumont, "The Conception of Kingship in Ancient India," *Contributions to Indian Sociology*, VI (December, 1962), pp. 48-77.

[44] Buddhagosha, *Path of Purification*, trans. by Bhikkhu Nanamoli, (Colombo: R. Semage, 1956), p. 460 (Visuddhimagga, Part II, Chapter XIII, Sec. 54).

and commentaries.[45] Moreover, taken together, these references reveal a coherent and consistent ideal.

The Cakkavatti is a Mahapurisa, a Great Being who has achieved that status through the merit which he has stored up during many previous lives. His birth is accompanied by a series of miracles and when he has reached the appropriate age his charisma calls forth the wheel which normally abides in the depths of the ocean, a wheel which is closely associated with the solar disc on the one hand and the Dhamma on the other.[46] In concert with the wheel which his charisma sets in motion, he proceeds to conquer the four continents and thereby establish his universal authority. He rules his empire with Dhamma and in so doing brings prosperity and happiness to his subjects. At his death the wheel returns to its abode in the depths of the ocean where it remains until a new Cakkavatti appears. In his kingdom his subjects erect a stupa over his remains and make appropriate offerings.

In this mythic cycle, though no cosmogony is involved, the emphasis on sacred time is very strong. The Cakkavatti ideal is associated with the ancient "Aryan" kings; that is to say, those who ruled in the first and most propitious period. In fact, the failure of later kings to live up to this ideal is looked upon as the cause of the degeneration which characterized the subsequent eras. It is also recognized, however, that Cakkavatti kings are not completely a phenomenon of the past; on the contrary, it is expected that a Cakkavatti king will appear once again to reestablish a society ordered in accordance with Dhamma. And, particularly in the later strata of the tradition, the appearance of such a figure who will reestablish proper order and harmony in the world becomes an important element in the Buddhist tradition, an element which exerts a strong influence on religious attitudes and has a significant impact on political affairs as well.

Alongside the pattern of sacred time a conception of sacred space is also built into the Cakkavatti cycle. The Cakkavatti is depicted as a cosmocrator whose conquest proceeded through the continents located at each of the four cardinal points, and whose rule radiated out from a central position either identified or closely associated with the central cosmic mountain of the Indian tradition, Mount Meru. In the later texts this connection between the Cakkavatti and the cosmological pattern of the four directions and Mount Meru comes increasingly to the fore and it plays a dominant role in the architectural symbolism which developed in conjunction with Buddhist kingship.[47]

The Cakkavatti, as the central figure in this great, symbolically depicted universe, is a sacred personage whose charismatic qualifications are second only to

[45] These references are given under the "Cakkavatti" entry in The Pali Text Society's Pali-English Dictionary, 1959.

[46] For a discussion of the wheel symbolism, see Ananda Kentish Coomaraswamy, *Elements of Buddhist Iconography* (Cambridge: Harvard University Press, 1935).

[47] See Mus, *Barabadur*, and Jeannine Auboyer, *Le Trône et son symbolisme dans l'Inde ancienne* (Paris: Presses Universitaires de France, 1949).

those of a Buddha. It is his personal charisma which not only calls forth the wheel from its normal abode in the depths of the ocean, but also draws the other classic treasures which crystalize his rule, the elephant, the horse, the jewel, the banker, and the general.[48] Moreover, his authority is established by a kind of heroic conquest, though it should be emphasized that this conquest is carried out by the power of Dhamma rather than by military force, and that as the conquest proceeds it meets with the enthusiastic approval of the lesser kings and local populations who make their submission. Finally, the rule which is established is seen as paternalistic rather than contractual, the basic model being that of a father whose actions are guided by a benevolent concern for the well being of his offspring.[49]

Like the Mahasammata, the Cakkavatti's function is the maintenance of order and justice, conceived in terms of Dhamma. In the case of the Cakkavatti, however, the element of benevolence is more explicit and his rule is replete with soteriological overtones. Even within the canonical tradition this is made explicit in at least two forms. On the one hand, a close association is made between the coming of the future Buddha (*Metteyya*) and the reign of the future Cakkavatti named Samkha, an association which is later developed in such a way that the two figures are often merged into one in which the Buddha elements and the Cakkavatti elements are inseparable. On the other hand, the veneration of the stupa of a Cakkavatti is advocated and recognized as a means whereby rebirth in heaven can be assured, thus presaging the later tradition in which the rebirth attained by such means leads more or less directly to the attainment of final release.[50]

Alongside the two strongly mythic strands connected with the first king (Mahasammata) and the great wheel-rolling Cakkavatti, the Dhamma tradition formulated in the canonical and semi-canonical literature also included ideals of kingship which were nearer to the actual political situation. For example, in the Nikayas, the most commonly expressed ideal is that of a *Dhammiko Dhammarājā*, "a righteous Lord of the Right, ruler of the four quarters, conqueror, guardian of the people's good" who has a great deal in common with a Cakkavatti but without necessarily being associated with the strong mythic elements which have gone into the conception of the latter.[51] Though it is assumed that, like all men, a Dhammaraja is born to his station because of his deeds in previous lives, this aspect is not particularly emphasized nor is there any special reference to the

---

[48] For one of the several references to this list, see *Dialogues of the Buddha III*. Vol. IV of *Sacred Books*, p. 60. (Dīgha Nikāya III, xxvi, 2-3).

[49] *The Book of the Kindred Sayings I*. Vol. VII of *Trans. Series*, p. 10. (Saṁyutta Nīkāya, i, 6, I, 2, No. 5).

[50] *Dialogues of the Buddha II*. Vol. III of *Sacred Books*, p. 157. (Dīgha Nikāya II, xvi, 143).

[51] The Dhammaraja ideal is discussed and the relevant texts are brought together by Balkrishna Gokhale in "Dhammiko Dhammaraja—A Study in Buddhist Constitutional Concepts," in *Indica: The Indian Historical Research Institute Silver Jubilee Commemoration Volume* (Bombay: n.p., 1963), pp. 161-165.

manner of his birth. His accession to the throne is assumed to be normal and
Buddhagosha explicitly declares that he is called Dhammaraja by virtue of the
fact that he assumed authority through rightful succession. He is depicted as
one who has mastered his own passions and who rules in accordance with a sound
knowledge of the traditions of Dhamma, of the principles and techniques of
power, and of the proper treatment of the various castes and groups of Sramanas.
He possesses the normal symbols of sovereignty—the umbrella, the slippers, the
diadem, the sword, and the fly-whisk—but not necessarily the mystic treasures
of the Cakkavatti. His rule goes beyond the maintenance of order and justice
because it encompasses a benevolence which expresses itself in compassionate
action taken for the welfare of his subjects; nevertheless, specifically soteriological overtones are muted and there is no indication that an ordinary Dhammaraja
receives the kind of religious veneration which is considered appropriate for a
Cakkavatti.

In some sections of the canon and in a large number of passages in the commentaries, more popular traditions concerning kingship are also incorporated into
the tradition. Particularly in the *Jātakas* the king's role in maintaining the
Dhamma is closely correlated with his power to assure the proper order in nature
and especially the appropriate amount of rainfall.[52] Moreover, the relationships
between the ruler and supernatural powers, both the more universal gods such as
Indra (Sakka) and more local deities such as the Nagas (who were generally
conceived in snake or half snake, half human form and closely related to the
rains) and the *Yakkhas* (who were often associated with trees and considered to
be the source of territorial authority and fertility) were taken into account and
in some cases emphasized.[53] In addition, the legends and folklore included in
this strata of the tradition provided a storehouse of popular wisdom concerning
political affairs as well as other aspects of life; and as a result they came to serve
as a kind of source book for later Buddhist kings and royal advisors involved in
the practical problems of day to day political existence.[54]

When the very large volume of the early Buddhist Dhamma literature is taken
into account, it is evident that the amount of material devoted to kingship and
political affairs is actually rather modest. Nevertheless, the presence of these
elements in the early tradition is significant in that it indicates that even among
the supposedly world-renouncing monks who were responsible for the preservation and extension of the Buddha's teaching, such matters constituted one important focal point of interest and concern. And what is more important for our

[52] *The Jātaka or Stories of the Buddha's Former Births*, ed. by E. B. Cowell, Vol. II
(7 vols.; Cambridge: The University Press, 1895), p. 252; (*Jātaka* n. 276, *Kurudhamma-
Jātaka*).

[53] The Nagas are discussed by Jean Philippe Vogel in his *Indian Serpent Lore: or the
Nagas in Hindu Legend and Art* (London: A. Probsthain, 1926). A discussion of the
Yaksas is found in Ananda Kentish Coomaraswamy, *Yaksas* (Washington: The Smith-
sonian Institution, 1928-31).

[54] For example, the *Jātakas* are utilized in Vajiranana, *Buddhist Attitudes*.

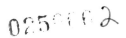

purposes, these elements are of crucial importance because they provided a commonly accepted, orthodox basis for the richer and more complex patterns of royal symbolism and political involvement which were developed during the subsequent periods of Buddhist history.

THE ASOKAN EXPERIENCE

Religious founders, as the term itself implies, were instrumental in the establishment of distinctively new, more or less permanent religious communities. And despite the differences which make each of these communities unique, they display a number of common features. In each case the community (for example, the *Ecclesia* in Christianity, the *Ummah* in Islam, and the *Saṅgha* in Buddhism) has been perceived both as a sacral reality which shares in the charisma of the Founder and his message, and as an historical, cultural institution through which that charisma is expressed and made available to the faithful. At the level of function each of these founded religious communities has assumed both a missionary and nurturing role; in every case these communities have taken up the task of proclaiming the meaning of the Founder's life and message, and at the same time have provided the social context within which the religious life, as each particular tradition has understood it, could be more effectively lived. Moreover, in terms of its development, each of these communities has begun with the Founder and the intimate circle of disciples which gathered around him, has passed through a phase in which the expansion of the community has been accompanied by the development of more permanent institutional forms, and has emerged, within a few centuries, as an integral element in one of the great civilizations, contributing to its life on the one hand, and being molded by its particular patterns of economic, political, and cultural order on the other.

Though the charismatic quality of the community has perhaps been less emphasized in the study of Buddhism than in the study of the other founded traditions, it has been present from the very beginning.[55] The Buddha's sacred activities were quickly extended and multiplied in the activities of the community. The Dhamma which was actualized and experienced through the Founder's preaching soon became actualized and experienced also in the common life which he shared with his disciples. Thus when the early Buddhists came to formulate the sacred realities which were fundamental for the religion, the Sangha was included alongside the Buddha and the Dhamma; "I take refuge in the Buddha, I take refuge in the Dhamma, I take refuge in the Sangha," became the basic confession of the Buddhist faith, a confession which to this day is repeated by Buddhist peoples wherever they are found.

In the scriptural accounts, the Buddhist community is depicted, from its in-

---

[55] In recent times the lacuna has been recognized. See, for example, the chapter on "Buddhism and the Samgha," in Joseph M. Kitagawa, *Religions of the East* (Philadelphia: Westminster, 1960), and Dutt, *Buddhist Monks.* In connection with Dutt's work, see my review in the *Journal of Religion*, Vol. XLIV, No. 3 (July, 1964).

ception, as a missionary community.[56] Very soon after the Buddha's first conver-
sions he sent those mendicants who had accepted his message out to convert
others; and their efforts contributed greatly to the expansion of the new sect.
Throughout the canonical period missionary preaching constituted one of the
major functions of the Buddha's mendicant followers including, it would seem,
not only the *bhikkhus* (members of the male order) but also the *bhikkhunīs*
(members of the order of nuns). Moreover, the laity soon became involved in
the missionary efforts and contributed mightily to its success. For example, it is
said that the daughter of the famous lay disciple Anathapindaka was responsible
for the conversion of her father-in-law's entire family and through her success
was instrumental in setting up a Buddhist center in the eastern country of
Anga.[57]

In the canonical accounts the nurturing function of the Sangha is depicted
with equal clarity. Though there are indications that at the earliest period, as
in most segments of Buddhist history, there were those who sought their own
salvation through isolation and solitude, the normative character of life within
the sacred community was never seriously questioned. For those most seriously
concerned with the attainment of salvation the normative pattern was that of a
mendicant wanderer living in the context of one of the Orders which the Buddha
had established and regulated in accordance with his Dhamma—either the Order
of bhikkhus which he had established for men or the Order of bhikkhunis which
he had established, rather reluctantly according to the scriptures, for women.[58]
For those men and women who were either unwilling or unable to give up this-
worldly activities, the accepted pattern was one of venerating the Buddha and
recognizing his authority, of understanding and following his Dhamma to the
greatest extent possible, and of providing the material support necessary for the
maintenance and well-being of the wanderers.[59] Though from one point of view
the way of the wanderers with its emphasis on renunciation was certainly considered to be more in accordance with the Path, the whole community was bound
together and the religious development of each individual was assured by the
reciprocal exchange between the mendicants and the laity—the mendicants,
through their example and preaching, brought the Dhamma to the laity, while
the laity, by the giving of material goods which itself constituted a discipline of
renunciation and benevolence, made it possible for the mendicants to maintain
their freedom from this-worldly involvement.

Though the specific phases in the development of the early Sangha are diffi-

---

[56] A detailed and well documented discussion of the early Buddhist missionary is contained in Nalinaksha Dutt, *Early History of the Spread of Buddhism and the Buddhist
Schools* (London: Luzac, 1925).

[57] Hendrik Kern, *Manual of Indian Buddhism* (Varanasi: Indological Book House,
1968).

[58] For a succinct, dependable discussion of the mendicant order and ideal, see LaMotte,
Histoire, pp. 58-70.

[59] For a discussion of the lay ideal, see *ibid.*, pp. 71-94.

cult to isolate and describe in detail, considerable progress had already been made even during the lifetime of the Founder. Joachim Wach was certainly correct when he emphasized that the religious founders were primarily interested in expressing their own unique and powerful religious experience and in proclaiming their message to others.[60] However, particularly for founders like Mohammed and the Buddha who had long public ministries, this primary interest became absolutely inseparable from the concern to guide and regulate the life of the communities which had accepted their leadership. In the case of the Buddha the practices which he followed and encouraged, and the advice which he gave when questions and dispute arose, provided the basic guidelines which were later codified, expanded, and adapted in accordance with changing conditions.

The traditions of the various sects are in agreement that during the first year after the Founder's death the leading mendicant disciples convened a council at Rajagaha, the city which at that time served as the capital of Magadha.[61] And according to these traditions this group of disciples, all of whom had been close to the Buddha during his lifetime, established authoritative collections of the Buddha's teachings concerning the Dhamma on the one hand, and the rules which he had established for regulating the life of the Order (the Vinaya) on the other. To be sure the great variations in the different accounts and the strongly legendary ring of many of the episodes have led some scholars, including such recognized authority as André Bareau, to deny its historicity.[62] However, even if the council as such did not actually take place, the fact which the accounts dramatized —namely the codification of the core of the Dhamma and the Vinaya by the early leaders of the mendicant Order—has been well established. For example, W. Pachow has published a careful comparative study of certain Vinaya texts which demonstrates the existence, within the first century after the Buddha's death, of a generally accepted *Pātimokkha* or collection of rules which governed the behavior of the bhikkhus and served as the basis for the bi-weekly ceremonies of confession around which much of their community life was organized.[63] Though a corresponding study of the Kammavaca segment of the Vinaya (containing the material concerning the functioning of the Order) has not yet been undertaken, the many parallels imbedded in the texts of the various schools suggest that in this area, too, a common core of tradition had become formulated and generally accepted within the first century or two after the Founder's death.[64]

[60] Wach, *Sociology*, p. 343.

[61] For a dated but still useful discussion of the councils, see Louis LaVallee Poussin, "Councils, Buddhist," in *Hastings Encyclopedia of Religion and Ethics*, 1916, IV, 179-185. Jean Przyluski, in his *Le Concile de Rajagraha: Introduction à l'histoire des canons et des sectes bouddhiques* (Paris: P. Geuthner, 1926), provides an interesting interpretation, though again the work is dated. A more recent discussion is found in André Bareau, *Les Premiers conciles bouddhiques* (Paris: Presses Universitaires de France, 1955).

[62] *Ibid.*, p. 145.

[63] W. Pachow, *Comparative Study of the Prātimoksha on the Basis of Its Chinese, Tibetan, Sanskrit and Pali Versions* (Santiniketan: Sino-Indian Cultural Society, 1955).

[64] LaMotte, *Histoire*, pp. 68-71, 181-197.

During the early centuries, before the various canonical traditions had become fixed, new elements began to intrude into the Vinaya which reveal an important shift in the structure of the community. As Sukumar Dutt has pointed out, these new elements demonstrate that the Order of wandering mendicants was gradually becoming divided into distinct groups associated with particular local residences. Largely as a result of the Buddhist emphasis on the mendicant's role in preaching the Dhamma "for the welfare of the many" and the laity's response in providing more permanent dwellings for the monks who served them, the mendicant order increasingly took the form of a monastic order encompassing a number of distinct local establishments, each with its own sense of identity and common life. By the end of the fourth century B.C., Buddhist monastic centers with their lay constituencies were spread through most of the expanded kingdom of Magadha, a kingdom which by this time had become the base from which a powerful dynasty founded by Chandragupta Maurya was in the process of establishing its rule over all of India.

Perhaps the most crucial single event in the development of the early Sangha occurred in the middle of the third century B.C. when Asoka Maurya, the grandson of Chandragupta, became a Buddhist. From the time of the Buddha and his contemporary, King Bimbisara, the relationship between the Buddhists and the Magadhan kings had been, as far as the records allow us to judge, positive. Though the form of polity which had been established for the internal life of the Buddhist Order was similar to the republican forms of the older tribal political organization and quite probably derived from them, the Sangha accepted the new monarchical and bureaucratic patterns as appropriate in the political sphere. And, as we have noted earlier, the Buddhist community, wherever it was possible, sought to gain the favor and support of the kings. The kings, from their side, tended to find Buddhism and the other new religions more attractive than the traditional Brahmanism partly, no doubt, because they could more easily be reconciled with the changing political and social ethos.[65] However, with the exception of such early kings as Bimbisara, who is depicted in the scriptures as a lay disciple and supporter of the Sangha, and his immediate successor Ajatasattu, who was reportedly converted just before the Buddha's death, there is no indication that during the Magadhan or early Mauryan period Buddhism was ever able to count a reigning monarch among its converts or to achieve anything like the status of a state religion.[66] Thus the conversion of a Mauryan king at the very time when the dynasty had reached the peak of its power and prestige, and the special favor and guidance which he provided throughout the remainder of his

[65] Certainly the Buddhist resistance to the religious valorization of caste played an important role. This is discussed by Drekmeier in his *Kingship.*

[66] The historical facts concerning the religious preferences and activities of Bimbarsa and Ajatasattu (like those of King Pasendi of Kosala whose commitment to the Buddha is also attested in the Pali scriptures) are actually very much in doubt. For example, the Jain scriptures present them as the active disciples and supporters of Mahavira. For a discussion of the problem, see N. Dutt, *Early History*, pp. 88-89.

reign, marked the beginning of a new phase in the history of the Buddhist community.[67]

The basic source of our knowledge concerning Asoka's conversion, his distinctive religious orientation, and his activities are the numerous edicts which he himself promulgated during his long reign, edicts which have been discovered, deciphered, and intensively studied by a number of modern philologists and Buddhologists.[68] In these messages addressed to his contemporaries—messages which constitute the oldest written documents concerning Buddhism which we possess —Asoka gives some important insight into his own religious development. He relates his conversion to his repentance for the bloody campaign which he had waged against the Kalingas during the early years of his reign. And he further relates that it was not until some years after his conversion that he became truly zealous in his religious commitment. For the most part, however, the edicts (all of which are dated after his religious commitment became firm) take the form of exhortations to his subjects to live in accordance with the Dhamma.[69]

In his assimilation of Buddhism, Asoka was frankly selective: "Whatever the Lord Buddha has said," Asoka announced, ". . . is of course well said. But it is proper for me to enumerate the texts which express the true Dhamma and which make it everlasting."[70] Though the correspondence between the texts which he then mentions and specific segments of the later canon remains a matter of conjecture, Asoka's conception of the "true Dharma" can be discerned in the edicts themselves. For him, at least insofar as his perspective is revealed in his public pronouncements, the Dhamma did not involve any identification between this existence and suffering, or any concern with the ultimate goal of Nibbana. The true Dhamma, as expressed in the edicts, was by no means the exclusive property of Buddhism, but rather an ideal fostered by all authentic religions. It was a moral teaching, an intercourse with the gods, and a meditational practice which was encouraged so that all men might benefit in this world and the next. For Asoka, in other words, the true Dhamma was a goal which could be actualized in the midst of the day to day personal and social life of his subjects.

Alongside Asoka's exhortations to his subjects the edicts contain numerous references to his own religiously oriented activities. They refer to his efforts to rule in accordance with Dhamma and to his restrictions on sacrifice and animal slaughter within his kingdom (however, significantly, capital punishment

[67] Among the books which discuss Asoka and his political and religious career, see Balkrishna Govind Gokhale's *Buddhism and Asoka*, with a Foreword by H. Heras (Baroda: Padmaja, 1948), and Romula Thapar's *Asoka and the Decline of the Mauryas* (London: Oxford University Press, 1961).

[68] For a translation of these edicts, see *The Edicts of Asoka*, trans. by N. A. Nikam and Richard McKeon (Chicago: University of Chicago Press, 1958).

[69] In the past some scholars have maintained that Asoka was not a Buddhist and that his Dhamma was not to be seen in the Buddhist context. However, this view is not justified by the texts and has been rejected by most contemporary scholars.

[70] McKeon and Nikam, *Edicts*, p. 66.

was never abolished). They mention his pilgrimage to Bodh Gaya (the place of the Buddha's Enlightenment) and to other pious tours, his sponsorship of "festivals of Dhamma" in his capital city, and his generous support of religious establishments. They indicate his concern for the unity and well-being of the Sangha and record that he appointed a number of *Dhamma-mahāmātras* (Ministers of the Dhamma) and that he gave them responsibility for overseeing and encouraging the activities of the Sangha and other similar religious communities. And finally, the edicts clearly indicate Asoka's missionary interest and refer to his specific efforts to spread the Dhamma both in India and in the Hellenistic kingdoms with which Mauryan India maintained contact.

The changes in the Buddhist community which came about as the result of Asoka's conversion, his open and universal perspective, and his many pious activities were both numerous and profound. Before his reign the Sangha had been a growing but still comparatively small sectarian community whose constituency was limited largely to the Magdhan regions of northeastern India. However, through the prestige which it acquired as a result of the great monarch's publicly proclaimed and dramatized personal commitment, through the encouragement and concrete assistance which he and his Dhamma-mahamatras were able to provide, and through the burst of missionary activity generated and guided by the new, more cosmopolitan spirit which he was able to instill, the community rapidly acquired large numbers of new converts and became established not only throughout most of the subcontinent, but in Ceylon as well. Through his influence, in other words, the Sangha became a pan-Indian community and the stage was set for its expansions into Central Asia, the Far East, and Southeast Asia.

Moreover, the memories and reflections of the community concerning Asoka and the meaning of his career were soon crystalized into a sacred biography expressing a new kind of Buddhist ideal.[71] In the traditional life story of the Founder the transformation from a life lived in ignorance to one lived in accordance with the Dhamma had come to be depicted in terms of the contrast between the sea of sensual pleasures in which Gautama had been immersed prior to the Great Renunciation and the calm equanimity characteristic of the Middle Way which he followed after his Enlightenment. In the sacred biography of Asoka, on the other hand, the transformation was presented in terms of a contrast between the terrible cruelties which were attributed to the monarch during the early portions of his career and the active piety and benevolence which are associated with all of his activities following his conversion. Thus, as a result of the Asokan experience, a second very specific and historically grounded model of Buddhist conversion and commitment emerged within the tradition. And quite clearly this second model was one which had particular relevance and meaning

[71] See Jean Przyluski, *La Légende de l'empereur Açoka (Açoka-Avadana) dans les textes indiens et chinois* (Paris: Paul Geuthner, 1923), and LaMotte, *Histoire*, pp. 261-283.

for those who were involved with the problems of worldly power and its responsibilities.[72]

And beyond this, the cycle of legends which grew up around the person of
Asoka provided a new, more fully developed model of the ideal Buddhist king.
In all of the various sectarian traditions Asoka came to be pictured as a Dhammaraja or Cakkavatti monarch who, in addition, was a devoted Buddhist layman. In
this connection the central position which was given to an account describing
his simultaneous construction of 84,000 stupas throughout his kingdom (an
action symbolizing the establishment of the Dhamma which, in its scriptural
form, was also divided into 84,000 segments) and his efforts, made successful
through the cooperation of the local Nagas and Yaksas, to animate each of the
stupas with an authentic portion of the Buddha's relics.[73] In addition, the biography emphasizes Asoka's beneficence toward the Sangha, focusing specifically on
the Pancavassa ritual in which the great king offered all of his goods, his family,
and ultimately his own person to the Order. And finally, in the Theravada versions the tradition also includes an account of Asoka's convening of a Buddhist
Council, so it is reported, confirmed the orthodox canon and its interpretation and describes the actions which he took to enforce its decisions. In
the sacred biography, then, Asoka is presented as a Dhammaraja or Cakkavatti
monarch whose devotion to the Buddha, the Dhamma, and the Sangha was complete and effective.

Thus in the post-Asokan period Buddhism emerged as a highly complex religious tradition in which the Three Jewels of the early tradition each had its
lay-oriented, but still intrinsically religious counterpart with which it was intimately associated and correlated. Alongside the figure of the Buddha which,
especially in the Theravada tradition, was coming to serve as a model for the
life of the bhikkhu, there developed the figure of Asoka who served as a model
for the life of the layman in general and for the Buddhist king in particular.[74]
Alongside and intertwined with the uniquely Buddhist Dhamma which was represented by the growing canonical tradition there developed the tradition of the
"true Dhamma" which could be actualized within the context of the ordinary
structures of social and political life. And in the same vein, there developed alongside the Buddhist Sangha, which was constituted by the Orders of monks and
nuns and the laymen and women who supported them, the ideal of a Buddhist
state governed by a pious monarch who modeled his rule after the example of

[72] For a perceptive discussion of this Asokan model as it developed in Ceylon, see the
essay by Bardwell Smith, *infra.*, Chapter Two.

[73] According to many versions of the biography Asoka, in a previous life, had offered
a piece of earth to the Buddha, thus evoking the latter's prediction that he would one day
become a great king devoted to the Dhamma. The significance of this "offering of the
earth" as a prefiguration of Asoka's career and specifically his construction of 84,000 stupas
is brilliantly discussed by Mus in *Barabadur.*

[74] For a discussion of the Buddha's life as a model for the bhikkhu see Levy, *Buddhism,*
chap. 1 and 2.

Asoka. Moreover, though this dual structure of the Buddhist tradition has often been overlooked, it is nevertheless true that the subsequent history of Buddhism can only be understood by taking into account the ethos created by the simultaneous veneration of the two careers (that of the Buddha and that of Asoka), the two coexisting and interacting ways of understanding the Dhamma (the Dhamma as expressed in the fullness of the canon on the one hand, and the "true Dhamma" on the other), and the two intimately interwoven patterns of community life (that of the Sangha and that of the Buddhist state).

In India itself, where Buddhism was unable to retain any long-term political or cultural hegemony, this dual structure, which became the hallmark of the Theravada ideal, gradually gave way to the new kind of syntheses which were achieved first by the Mahayanists and later by the Mantrayanists.[75] However in Ceylon, where Buddhism succeeded in establishing itself as a truly national religion, the dual, Theravada-type pattern has persisted through more than two millenia of turbulent religious and political history. To be sure, this "orthodox" pattern has been seriously challenged at various points in Sinhalese history by the Mahayana and Mantrayana orientations within Buddhism itself, by the pressures toward Hinduization which have been exerted almost continuously from South India, and in more recent times by the impact of the European powers and the closely correlated drive toward modernization. And it is also true that many of these encounters served to enrich the tradition in certain respects and in many instances forced serious adaptations and modifications.[76] All this having been said, however, it still remains that the basic ethos of the Buddhism which emerged from the Asokan experience, and particularly its emphasis on the equal and complimentary importance of the two wheels of Dhamma, continue to mold the ideals and activities of the Sinhalese Sangha and, to some extent at least, the ideals and orientation of the contemporary Sinhalese state.[77]

---

[75] Though a discussion of the problem would take us well beyond the limits set for the present paper it is perhaps worth mentioning that the Mahayana and Mantrayana developments can be greatly illuminated by taking into account the way in which they presuppose, but at the same time transform, the established pattern.

[76] A good discussion is found in Walpola Rahula, *History of Buddhism in Ceylon: The Anuradhapura Period; 3rd Century B.C.—10th Century A.D.* (Second edition, Colombo: M. D. Gunasena, 1966).

[77] Perhaps the best account is found in Heinz Bechert, *Buddhismus, Staat und Gesellschaft in den Ländern des Theravāda-Buddhismus*, Vol. I (Frankfurt and Berlin: Alfred Metzner, 1966).

The Ideal Social Order as Portrayed in the Chronicles of Ceylon

BARDWELL L. SMITH

[*Suṇātha me. Suṇātha me.*] Listen to me, I shall relate the Chronicle of the Buddha's coming to the island, the arrival of the relic and the Bo-Tree and the advent of the Buddha's religion in the island and of the doctrine of the teachers who made the collection as well as of the advent of the chief of men . . . . Listen to the eulogy of the island, incomparable, that which deals with the lineage of the best dwellers, original, unrivalled and well-narrated, handed down by the elect, described by the noblest and adored by the righteous.[1]

So begins the earliest Pāli chronicle of Ceylon, an authoritative historical poem, written in the late fourth or early fifth century A.D. by an unknown author. It is the attempt of this essay to discern the image or concept of an ideal social order which lies buried, yet remains assumed, in the pages of the two primary chronicles of the Sinhalese people, the *Dīpavaṃsa* and the *Mahavaṃsa*, which together trace the history of *Laṅkā* (Ceylon) from the advent of Vijaya in 483 B.C. down to modern times. In line with the chronicles themselves, the focus here is upon the classical period of Sinhalese Buddhism from its inception in the third century B.C. to the fall of its early capital Anurādhapura in 1029 A.D. For primary material the essay limits itself to these chronicles, with a few exceptions, though examination of various other sources has helped fill out the picture.[2] These other materials amplify but do not essentially alter the picture found within the Sinhalese chronicles.

Immediately, the question of historiography arises: how is one to treat source material such as the *Dīpavaṃsa* and the *Mahāvaṃsa*, material which is more normative than descriptive, more poetic than the writing of history as we now know it? It is difficult enough knowing how the chroniclers imagined the history of Buddhism, let alone discovering what the facts were during this period. B. C. Law may not be far wrong in saying about the chronicles that

---

[1] *Dīpavaṃsa*, edited by B. C. Law (Maharagama, Ceylon: Saman Press, 1959), pp. 129-130.

[2] The Venerable Walpola Rahula cites the main sources on which he based his *History of Buddhism in Ceylon*: namely, the Pāli Scriptures, the Aśokan Edicts, the Ceylon Inscriptions, the Pāli Commentaries, Sinhalese Folk-tales, and miscellaneous works in Pāli and Sinhalese. Besides his work, most of the secondary sources used in this essay also deal extensively with this material. While considerable work remains to be done on the whole period in question, present scholarship is based upon a wealth of sources which corroborate and supplement the story told within the chronicles. Cf. Rahula, *History of Buddhism in Ceylon* (Colombo: M. D. Gunasena and Co., second edition, 1966), p. xix.

"just as the religious motive cannot be divorced from the cultural advancement, so the patriotic motive cannot be separated from the promotion of the general cause of piety."[3] Clearly, this is history written with a motive. It is *Heilsgeschichte*. It is the sacred history of a people destined with a sacred mission, namely, to maintain the purity of the *Dhamma* in a world of impermanence and self-seeking.[4] As one enters the world of these chronicles, one enters a world not unlike that of the Old Testament, a world in which bare fact was always less important than what the fact signified. In any case, this is interpreted history. It is didactic by nature, sometimes moralistic. By definition, it is ethnocentric; history itself revolves around the history of this people. At its worst, it becomes fiercely judgmental, condoning savagery if done in the cause of mission. But, in all of this, one is walking upon familiar ground, as no people recording their ancient past (or their present, for that matter) are free of self-justification. As with wisdom literature in general, whether in the Old Testament, the *Jātakas*, or as found within the Sinhalese chronicles, the primary intent is twofold: to provide paradigmatic models for the present and the future and to engage in anamnesis or cultic reawakening of a people to the high points in its past and present destiny.

Any piece of literature can be judged by what it excludes as well as by the bias it reveals. Clearly, the interests of the chroniclers acted as a sieve which ignored much that we would like to know. As Rahula stressed about these writings, "secular history is subservient to religious history."[5] Here is in no sense a history of Ceylon. It is at most source material for the history of Buddhism in Ceylon, especially for the *Mahāvihāra* bhikkhus, material comprised of myth, fable, legend, and history interpreted through tradition. Law is right, however, in saying that "germs of historical truth" are "buried deep under a mesh of absurd fables and marvellous tales."[6] Or, to put it differently: "The garb in which these fantasies appear says more perhaps of the cultural and social circumstances of a people than its recorded history. To discard legend, and myth, and fairy tale would just as much rob one of one's most valuable sources of information about a people as to reject its art and literature as unimportant."[7]

With this preface in mind the essay proceeds to sketch out the central ingredients of an ideal social order as this emerges from the richly varied stories, accounts, and interpretations which comprise the chronicles in question. In the process four categories will be explored: first, the sense of continuity which is

[3] B. C. Law, *On the Chronicles of Ceylon* (Calcutta: *Journal of the Royal Asiatic Society of Bengal,* 1947), p. 43.

[4] "For more than two thousand years the Sinhalese have been inspired by the ideal that they were a nation brought into being for the definite purpose of carrying the torch lit by the Buddha." D. G. Vijayavardhana, *Dharma-Vijaya (Triumph of Righteousness) or The Revolt in the Temple* (Colombo, Sinha Publications, 1953), p. 3.

[5] Rahula, *op. cit.,* p. xxiv.

[6] B. C. Law, Introduction to the *Dīpavamsa, op. cit.,* p. 5.

[7] E. F. C. Ludowyk, *The Footprint of the Buddha* (London: George Allen and Unwin Ltd., 1958), p. 11.

present throughout, continuity of Indian tradition with Sinhalese tradition, of earliest Buddhism with later emerging forms, of popular religious expression with the *Buddha-sāsana* itself; second, the awareness of evil and the ever-present sensed threat of disorder in relationship to which the concept of kingship becomes an ambiguous reality; third, the concept of *Dharma-vijaya* (of conquest through righteousness, not force) as developed originally by Asoka and as reaffirmed by the *Saṅgha* in Ceylon providing the basis for symbiosis between monarch and Sangha and between monarch and people, establishing the normative pattern for Sinhalese kings from the earliest days; and fourth, the assumed interconnection between what happens in society and what occurs in the cosmos at large, alongside the depiction of an ideal king and the configurations of the City of Righteousness as these in some sense presage, in some sense prepare men for, the ultimate goal of *Nibbāna*.

I. THE SENSE OF CONTINUITY

From start to finish in the chronicles one is kept aware of historic continuities, whether those of royal clans and families, apostolic succession (*ācariya-paramparā*) within the early Sangha, the lineage of the Buddha himself, or whether those stemming from cultural contact and productive of new forms.[8] Only a detailed study could do justice to Ceylon's cultural indebtedness to both Aryan and Dravidian India. The basic social and political institutions, the vast majority of literary and art forms, the gift of the *Dharma*[9] itself all passed from the subcontinent over centuries to Ceylon. The story is a complex and fascinating one in its own right. Only certain highlights can be touched here.

One thread which provides both meaning and threat to Sinhalese self-consciousness is the ever-recurring pressure of Tamil invasion and occupation. Neither the present scene in Ceylon nor its lengthy history can be understood without a vivid awareness of the ambivalent relationship between these two peoples, now one of alliance and reciprocity, now of embittered hostility. Over the centuries it was essentially the latter which prevailed, reaching epic proportions in the chronicles and draining the economy and manpower seriously at many points in time. The "myth had been cultivated under Duttugemunu [Duṭṭha-Gāmiṇī, 101-77 B.C.] and was writ into Sinhalese political tradition" that the Tamils were Lanka's natural enemy.[10] Whether from the Pandyans, the

---

[8] The discontinuities are no less present but by comparison during the classical period seem subdued. One observes them in the breakdown of dynasties, in the resolute but abortive resistance by orthodoxy of heretical doctrines, in the gradual decline of Sinhalese civilization itself beginning in the thirteenth century, to mention only three.

[9] In an essay dealing in part with the influence of Indian thought upon Sinhalese it is inevitable that both Sanskrit and Pali terms be used and that the same term be rendered first in one, then in the other (e.g., *Dharma; Dhamma*). The spelling used depends upon the context.

[10] "Thus it was that a people who had very close cultural relations with each other were cast politically in the role of antagonists. By retaining their independence, the Sinhalese were enabled to develop their distinctive strand of civilization, though they owed

Colas, or the Pallavas, the threat never disappeared. By invasion, by infiltration, by being used increasingly as mercenaries, and through intermarriage, the Tamil presence made itself known, until finally in 1325 they had established an independent kingdom in the north of Ceylon.

Far more important for our present subject, however, were the Brahmanical influences upon Sinhalese culture and religion. Following the lead of Asoka in his tolerance of other religions, Buddhism displayed consistent openness toward Hindu institutional forms and devotional practices, absorbing or converting them in the process. Wilhelm Geiger rightfully underscores the fallaciousness of separating too radically Buddhism from Brahamanism.[11] The latter was regarded more as preparatory to the former than antagonistic. The Hindu gods, Indra (Sakka) especially, are invoked throughout as guardian and protective figures who further the Buddha's cause in Lanka. As Theravada Buddhists typically indicate, the gods play no role in the attainment of Nibbana.[12] As in the Buddha's words, one must remain an island unto oneself;[13] no one can cross over for another. If this qualification is maintained, then orthodoxy has no quarrel with divine assistance. In the *Mahāvaṃsa* the Buddha himself speaks to Sakka, prior to entering *parinibbāna*, recording his last will and testament, namely, that Vijaya, his followers, and Lanka be protected by the gods.[14] Throughout the establishing and maintaining of the Dhamma in Ceylon, the path is cleared and facilitated for the Buddha's followers by the heavenly hosts, whether this be in the consecrating of the nation's rulers, the arrival of the relics, the coming of the Bodhi-tree, or the wars against enemies. To put this into perspective with the core of the Buddha's teaching, one may posit a correspondence between this kind of assistance rendered by the gods and that afforded by Sinhalese kings. While different in substance and in degree, ideally both help to create the climate in which the Dhamma may thrive. In essence, then, the gods are converted to the Buddha's cause, revealing the cosmic nature of its scope.

With respect to the Brahmanical influences upon the Sinhalese concept of kingship and the political order, an entire study would be profitable.[15] Suffice

much to Dravidian influences." Cf. S. Arasaratnam, *Ceylon* (Englewood Cliffs, New Jersey: Prentice-Hall, Inc., 1964), p. 60.

[11] Wilhelm Geiger, *Culture of Ceylon in Medieval Times* (Wiesbaden: Otto Harrassowitz, 1960), p. 176.

[12] The attainment of arahantship through beholding the miraculous, "with believing and joyous heart," need not be held inconsistent with the above, as this stage precedes that of final extinction. It should be noted, however, that the chronicles frequently record the mass attainment of arahantship in this manner. Cf. *Mahāvaṃsa*, Wilhelm Geiger, tr. (London: Luzac and Company, Ltd., 1964), p. 217, for one example.

[13] *Cakkavatti-Sīhanāda Suttanta*, T. W. Rhys Davids, ed. (London: Luzac and Company, Ltd., 1965), pp. 74-75.

[14] *Mahāvaṃsa*, p. 55. The responsibility is then delegated by Sakka to Visnu.

[15] Several studies have dealt with this subject in part, though no exhaustive treatment has yet appeared. Geiger's work mentioned above and an interesting article by B. G. Gokhale, entitled "Early Buddhist Kingship," are two among many. The latter will be discussed later.

it to indicate here the continuity which is apparent, without elaborating upon its configurations. Of immense symbolic importance is the fact that Sinhalese kings retained both the central ingredients of the Hindu coronation ceremony (*abhiseka*) and the institution of the *purohita* or domestic chaplain to the throne. While partly ceremonial or cultic in form, these provided also a perspective and dimension which conveyed extensive Brahmanical culture in the process. It is possible to make too much of this channel, as discontinuities in the transformation of the caste system and in other areas are important, but the tie with Aryan tradition which this provided is unmistakable. Linguistic, religious, familial, economic, and political elements passed regularly from Indian to Sinhalese soil, in the end inadvertently contributing to a "Sanskritization" of this culture and to an increasing, almost dominant, Hindu influence in the Gupta period and beyond.

One aspect of the purohita-monarch relationship which needs further exploration is the degree to which this helped introduce and institutionalize *Realpolitik* procedures and policies. In what ways, for instance, whether through the king's chaplain directly or not, were policies shaped by the strategems of Kautalya's *Arthaśāstra*, the Machiavellian manual of Indian regents? Paul Mus, in commenting upon the Theravada scene as a whole, raises this same question: "Even in ancient history has not State Politics in the area derived its inspiration more from the pragmatic tradition of power developed in neighboring Hindu Kingdoms, than from so aloof and retiring a Church?"[16] While somewhat rhetorical in nature, for he is equally concerned in this essay to show how Buddhism has expressed itself politically, his question suggests the impact Indian statecraft had upon policy-making in Theravadin societies generally, an impact which does not go unnoticed in the Sinhalese chronicles. The teaching of *nīti*, or statecraft, to the future King Dhatusena by his uncle is one case in point.[17] While not at the hands of a royal chaplain, in fact the uncle was a bhikkhu, the explicit mentioning of a ruler's need for such knowledge and training is both symptomatic of the internecine and foreign adversaries each king faced *and* symbolic of the Sangha's recognition that, this side of *Metteyya's* coming, heads of state do not rule by righteousness alone.

The final continuity to be mentioned is, for our purposes, the most important. It is that which links the Buddha and early Buddhism in India to the advent and confirmation of the Dhamma in Ceylon. The *Dīpavaṃsa* and the *Mahāvaṃsa* both open with an account of the *Tathāgata's* three visits to Lanka in the first eight years of his enlightenment. These events are not recorded in the Pali Canon but, alongside the Buddha's invoking of divine protection for Lanka, serve to set the stage in Sinhalese self-consciousness for its efforts to preserve uninterruptedly the purity of the Master's doctrine. Even this continuity is

---

[16] Paul Mus, Preface to *Buddhist Backgrounds of the Burmese Revolution* by E. Sarkisyanz (The Hague: Martinus Nijhoff, 1965), p. vii.

[17] *Cūlavaṃsa*, I, Wilhelm Geiger, tr. (Colombo: Ceylon Government Information Department, 1953), p. 30.

set in a Brahmanic context, for it is an astute Brahmin, the youngest of 108 consulted to interpret the meaning of the thirty-two "distinctive marks" (*lakkhaṇāni*) upon the infant Siddhattha, who predicts he is to become a Buddha, not a Universal Monarch (*Cakkavatti*).[18] And, it is a converted Brahmin, Dasaka, who inherits the apostolic mantle from Upali as the chain of succession proceeds from the Buddha, over two centuries, to Mahinda (Asoka's bhikkhu son) and from him to the Sangha as it roots itself in Ceylon. Coupled with the placing of Gotama himself in the lineage of *Mahāsammata*, the Great Sage-King "in the beginning of this age of the world,"[19] one has a distinct sense of the new doctrine and religion being presented as "a repetition of the ancient archeotype."[20] The present is vividly connected with the past, providing both for legitimacy and for remembrance of the tradition's roots. One has the sense also of how the Mahavihara chroniclers, writing several centuries later in a time of political and sectarian turmoil, are engaging in the task of recreating their own tradition.[21]

Aside from the cosmic and existential significance of tracing its origins to the Buddha, the key ingredients in the Sangha's authentication of its mission were doctrinal, devotional and political. With respect to *doctrine*, the history of Sinhalese Buddhism could be written from the standpoint of the interplay between the Theravadins and the whole Acariyavada (or heterodox) movement with its many sects, beginning with the Vesali monks at the time of the Second Council and continuing to the present. Early in the chronicles one is exposed to the conciliar movement, arising in Buddhism upon the Tathagata's passing and reaching its peak at the time of Asoka with the "compilation of the true Dhamma."[22] Throughout the *Mahāvaṃsa* one is aware not only of the obvious tensions existing between the Mahavihara bhikkhus and those in various sects co-existing with them in Anuradhapura but also of the subtle influences these sects, especially those affected by Mahayana ideas, had upon the *Theriya Nikāya* or orthodox strain. Some of these influences will be examined later. It only needs indicating here that Buddhism, like all great religious traditions, has dealt with difficulty with the problems of schism, sectarianism, and heresy. While exceedingly tolerant of other faiths, popular and sophisticated, and while extraordinarily able to incorporate and transform indigenous elements, Sinhalese Buddhism has persistently felt threatened by the specter of heretical movements from within. In the words of G. P. Malalasekere: "To the assaults of open opponents the Buddhist displays the calmest indifference, convinced that in its undimin-

---

[18] As we shall see later, through Mahāyāna influence he becomes both.

[19] *Mahāvaṃsa*, p. 10.

[20] Ludowyk, *op. cit.*, p. 88.

[21] *Ibid.* E. W. Adikaram in his *Early History of Buddhism in Ceylon* shows how bhikkhus are encouraged in their efforts to lead a pure life by being reminded that they are "descended from the unbroken line of Mahāsammata," are grandsons of "the great king Suddhodana" and are younger brothers of Rahulabhadda. Cf. Adikaram (Colombo: M. D. Gunasena and Co., Ltd., 1946), p. 126.

[22] *Mahāvaṃsa*, p. 49.

ished strength his faith is firm and inexpungable; his vigilance is only excited by the alarm of internal dissent, and all his passions are aroused to stifle the symptoms of schism."[23]

The *devotional* ingredients continuous with earliest Buddhism likewise play a major part in the chroniclers' saga. If continuity of doctrine can be traced through the councils, the apostolic succession, and the safeguarding of the Dhamma's purity by the Sangha, the sense of wonder and joy released through awareness of the Buddha's gift are enlivened through anamnesis and celebration. While images of the Buddha himself came only after centuries, his sensed presence was (in the testimony of the chronicles) from the beginning. The words voiced by Mahinda, as he yearns for his homeland and the holy places associated with Gotama, are the words of tradition: "If we behold the relics we behold the Conqueror."[24] As the story of Sinhalese Buddhism could be told through the interplay between orthodoxy and sectarianism, it could be told with equal profit by discussion of the Buddhist sense of adoration. Without question, the high points in the reigns of Ceylon's two greatest kings during the Anuradhapura period, which spanned fourteen centuries,[25] were the arrival and enshrinement of relics from India. Kings Devanampiyatissa and Dutthagamini are remembered as epic figures for many reasons, but the coming of the relics confirmed and consecrated not only their reigns but the nation itself in the judgment of the Sinhalese chronicles. As the planting of the Bodhi-tree symbolized the spreading of the doctrine from its land of origin, the receiving of the relics confirmed the Buddha's authority in the land. With both gifts, the results were miraculous and enduring; the chronicles spare no words in telling of the wonder: "When the prince [Dutthagāmaṇi] saw the celestial parasol, the celestial perfumes, and the rest, and heard the sound of celestial instruments of music and so forth, albeit he did not see the Brahma-gods he, rejoicing and amazed at the miracle, worshipped the relics, with the offering of a parasol and investing them with the kingship of Laṅkā."[26]

The problem of true authority and kingship leads directly to the third ingredient of continuity established by the Sangha in the doctrine's spread to Ceylon, namely, the *political.* This was preeminently crystallized in the reconsecration of Devanampiyatissa by envoys from Asoka. The *Mahāvaṃsa* records that at the first consecration of King Tissa "many wonders came to pass . . . treasures and jewels that had been buried deep rose to the surface," and that "all this was the effect of Devanampiyatissa's merit."[27] Out of gratitude he sends these treasures to King Asoka, a friend though they had never met. In return, Asoka sends

<hr />

[23] G. P. Malalasekere, *The Pali Literature of Ceylon,* (London: Royal Asiatic Society of Great Britain and Ireland, 1928), p. 54. He goes on to document the measures used to suppress this dissent. It is only fair to indicate that the attacks were reciprocal.

[24] Mahāvaṃsa, p. 116.

[25] 377 B.C. - 1029 A.D.

[26] *Mahāvaṃsa,* p. 216.

[27] *Ibid.,* pp. 78-79.

"all that was needful for consecrating a king" and with these the message of his having taken refuge in the Three Jewels (*Triratna*), urging his friend: "Seek then even thou, O best of men converting thy mind with believing heart refuge in these best of gems!"[28] It is a delightful passage, punctuated by directions to his envoys: "Consecrate my friend yet again as king."[29]

In these words and actions are symbolized the line of continuity from the imperial majesty of Asoka to the small island of Lanka *and* from where the doctrine arose to where it was destined to flourish. In time, Anuradhapura became the Sinhalese counterpart of Pataliputta, the great capital of Asoka. In a sense, when Mahinda came to Ceylon, he brought not simply a religion but "a whole civilization at the height of its glory," its concepts of art and architecture, its language and literature, even its very alphabet.[30] But from the standpoint of establishing Buddhism's legitimacy there could have been no greater safeguard than imperial sanction. As more than one commentator has pointed out and as the chronicles themselves infer with frequency, royal support is a two-edged sword. Established religion is not always, if ever, true religion. In any case, while it cannot be said that the Buddha's doctrine entered Ceylon for the first time with Asoka's envoys or even with Mahinda, it can be dated as a state or court religion with the second consecration of Tissa. At this juncture and in what unfolded with Asoka's follow-up mission through his son Mahinda two lines of succession merged and Sinhalese Buddhism came into being. These lines were those of *rāja-paramparā* and *thera-paramparā*, of royal and ecclesiastical legitimacy. In the process were brought into new relationship two central realities within the sasana, both essential historically to Theravada at large, that of the patron-monarch and that of the bhikkhu-sangha.

The image of Asoka loomed larger with time. Legends about the great king were circulated soon after his death (later collected in the Sanskrit *Aśokāvadana*), but their full impact only hit Ceylon about the time the chronicles were being written.[31] It is evident not only from the prominence given Asoka in the early part of the scenario but, as one reads further, it becomes even clearer that the Sinhalese model for kingship, as well as for the *upāsaka* in general, is based upon the image these legends afford of the great king. A major feature of what is to be sensed in the figure of Asoka is the tradition's superimposing of the two great Kings: the Buddha and the Universal Monarch. This only becomes manifest as

[28] *Ibid.*, p. 80.

[29] *Ibid.* Rahula makes the point that it was Asoka who also conferred the honorific term *Devānampiya* ("beloved of the gods") upon the Sinhalese King. While used in India even before Asoka, it had not been used as a prefix in Ceylon prior to this time. It was a term used of Asoka himself and therefore reinforces the sense of continuity. Cf. Rahula, *op. cit.*, p. 27.

[30] Rahula, *op cit.*, pp. 59-60. Seven centuries later, the tide had reversed itself and various like Buddhaghosa in the fifth century A. D. made their way to Ceylon to translate the Sinhalese commentaries into the Magadhi tongue and make its insight available beyond Lanka. With this event, symbolically, the wheel had turned full circle, so to speak.

[31] Sarkisyanz, *op. cit.*, p. 33.

one perceives the emergence of the Cakkavatti figure in later centuries. But suggestions of it are apparent in the first part of the *Mahāvaṃsa*, i.e., by the early sixth century. It was this image which, however variously construed, became the paradigm for each king of Lanka. It was the image both of the Universal Monarch (the Cakkavatti) and of the Great Man (the *Mahāpurisa*, the Buddha himself) fused into one.

> It is in this light that the emblem of the sacred footprint should be considered. It could be taken as the symbol of the imprint of the civilization of the mainland on its island neighbor. It is more, it is the token of the Great Man. Incomprehensible though the devotion shown to it may be, its real value lies in its plain significance too—the veneration Indian civilization has always paid to the great human being, the sage who through his wisdom enables humankind to free itself from ignorance.[32]

II. THE THREAT OF DISORDER

If there was a tendency for the image of Asoka to assume Cakkavatti proportions, there was also the constant insistence that this flower had emerged from the mud of human rapacity. Injustice is done to Asoka himself if one forgets what preceded his transformation. Indeed, this is central to his appeal as an ideal monarch; it is what makes identification with him by ruler after ruler believable. It is not simply the majesty of his imperial power which appeals; it is the attraction of power tamed and made righteous. We have here then an ideal of righteous and benevolent power in tension with self-seeking power as most men know it. The total image of Asoka contains both; "his cruelty and his piety"[33] must each be seen in order to comprehend his paradigmatic attraction and to discern what Buddhism is saying about man. Asoka, therefore, is not only the Great Man (the Mahapurisa); he is also Everyman. Asoka, the wicked and cruel (*Candāśoka*), becomes Asoka, the just and righteous (*Dhammāśoka*).[34] In one human life we have the crystallization of two contrasting images, that of classic brutality and that of classic tolerance. As is well known, what unites these two is the sense of horror and repentance which were Asoka's following the carnage of the Kalingas by his troops. It was this decisive event and its aftermath which, as tradition reports, impels him toward Dharma-vijaya, conquest through righteousness rather than by force. Here is not the renunciation of power but its transformation. It is this *metanoia* which makes him a compelling model throughout the Theravada world.

[32] Ludowyk, *op. cit.*, p. 23. The reference in the first sentence is to the Buddha's footprint on Adam's Peak in south-central Ceylon.

[33] *Ibid.*, p. 61.

[34] *Mahāvaṃsa*, p. 42. As we shall see later when considering the concept of an Ideal King, the epithets for such a figure are myriad. *Dhammarājā* is one; *Priyadarśi rājā* is another. The latter means "one who sees to the good of others," i.e., the prototype of benevolence. Cf. *The Edicts of Asoka*, ed. and tr. by N. A. Nikam and Richard McKeon (Chicago: University of Chicago Press, 1959), pp. 25-26.

That this is one of one piece with the experience of Prince Siddhattha makes the model all the more authentic. The latter's exposure to the existence of suffering was transmuted upon enlightenment into insight regarding its causes. The Buddha's vision of human nature in the grips of self-aggrandizement was profoundly realistic. This insight is intrinsic to Buddhism, sparing it from becoming naive about man's capacity for evil. While the Buddha's teachings added new depth to this vision, it may in retrospect be seen as continuous with the overall Indian analysis of man's plight. This is made graphic in the *Cakkavatti-Sihanāda Suttanta* within the Pali Canon which presents two apocalyptic images —of life under the rule of evil and of life ruled by Dhamma.[35] The one is a picture of injustice, disorder, and confusion; the other portrays liberation and reciprocity. Both are extended images of the human potential, kept in balance as with Asoka. From the Buddhist standpoint, neither one can be fully appreciated except in relationship to the other. It does little good trying to make sense of the Ideal King concept or that of the City of Righteousness (as portrayed in *The Questions of King Milinda*), even of the king-Sangha relationship, unless one takes seriously the note of realism sounded by the tradition. This note is nowhere more vivid than in the Sinhalese chronicles.

The opening words of the *Mahāvaṃsa*, in fact, state the chronicler's intent throughout, namely, that these passages awaken in the reader "serene joy and emotion" (*pasāda* and *saṃvega*): joy, blissfulness and satisfaction in the doctrine of the Buddha; and emotion, horror, and recoil from the world and its misery.[36] Similarly, each chapter ends with the same refrain, "compiled for the serene joy and emotion of the pious." If one is encouraged toward ecstatic euphoria by some passages and events, one is brought into sharp confrontation with more somber reality by others. Sobriety alternates with the sense of wonder in powerful juxtaposition. One is never led too far in either direction. If tempted to place evil outside one's community, it springs up in one's midst. Though stylized and moralistic at times, the language of the chronicles does not romanticize the human predicament. Sinhalese man, like man in the Old Testament, is portrayed with an honesty which is refreshing. At the very times you would expect the picture to leave out the darker hues they suddenly appear. Indeed, profane history portrayed in this manner becomes a subject for meditation (*kammaṭṭhāna*), showing not only life's impermanence but man's anxiety in the face of it.[37] In the words of one commentator: "What better theme for meditation than the crimes and follies of mankind. If history had no other lesson to teach, scanning its pages or rather hearing its sad stories of the death of its

---

[35] Set into the poetic framework of the four cycles of history (the four *yūgas*) we find the beginnings of a new historiography which, while retaining much of the Brahmanic perspective, points forward to the expectation of the Buddha Metteyya and time's fulfillment, not unlike what occurred in later Hinduism as well, in the *bhakti-magga* of Ramanuja and others.

[36] *Mahāvaṃsa*, p. 1.

[37] Rahula, *op. cit.*, p. 162.

kings, was to fortify oneself anew in the knowledge of the transiency of all things, and to savour, by contrast, the joy of the mind directed towards the Four Noble Truths."[38]

Basic to the Buddhist understanding of evil is their apprehension about the consequences of disorder. The threat of anarchy and chaos is ever-present in the chronicler's mind. While the identity of the *yakkhas* has often been debated, whether demons or non-human tutelary deities or ancestors of the present *Väddās*, it is more probable that tradition has invested them with even profounder symbolism. If aborigines in some sense, they represent the aboriginal spirit of man which lurks not far beneath the surface, the protean fount of fear and self-enslavement which, unless stilled, infects all his acts and colors every thought. While on one level the Buddha's coming to Lanka can be interpreted as freeing it from yakkha control, making it ready for the Sinhalese race, on another level it becomes exorcism of the demonic from man himself. As with the Marcan account in the New Testament of the Gerasene demoniac, one senses here the removal of that which can be lodged in any man.[39] When confronted by the Buddha, the yakkhas, "overwhelmed by fear," beseech "the fearless Vanquisher to release them from terrors."[40] Hypostasized into imaginary figures the yakkhas may represent tradition's own realistic fear of man's proclivity toward disorder and evil. In any case, sensitivity toward the demonic remains a permanent ingredient of Sinhalese consciousness. Though the yakkhas are released from their distress and are converted to the Buddha's cause, the chronicles record the on-going turmoil within and between men. Three centuries after the Master's visit, Mahinda, in the *Dīpavaṃsa* account, reflects about his own mission to Lanka in conversation with Sakka (the lord of the gods) and makes a statement which history proves to be double-edged: "Tambapaṇṇi [Ceylon] is covered and closed with the overclouding darkness of ignorance and of worldly existence, it is destroyed by jealousy and selfishness. . . . It has obtained the wrong path, it has gone astray, it is entangled like a ball of string and covered with blight."[41] Such a statement can be double-edged, for to Sinhalese nationalism the liberation from fear and ignorance can seem to be a *fait accompli*, an unrepeatable act making Lanka for all time "fit for human habitation,"[42] while to more honest self-reflection it may appear as but a foretaste of what must occur throughout time.

The evidence is overwhelming in the chronicles that the latter appraisal is more basic. Consistent with the tension found in the image of Asoka, the image of the island kingdom one perceives in these pages is twofold: as the archetype of delusion and as the paragon of enlightenment. What one finds here is a mixture of both in the nation's history. If the forces of evil are stilled in some,

[38] Ludowyk, *op. cit.*, pp. 107-108.
[39] Mark 5:1-20.
[40] *Mahāvaṃsa*, p. 4.
[41] *Dīpavaṃsa*, p. 201.
[42] *Ibid.*, p. 191.

they are rampant in others. In all, however, they are realities acknowledged and underscored. As Vijaya, forebear of the race, was wild in his conduct before taming, so each man needs separation from ignorance and self-possession. The centuries of Sinhalese history, like that of each people, are written in blood. Intrigue follows intrigue. Parricides appear *in seriatim*. Subversion, treason, infamy, and unrest unfold in ritualistic regularity. The threat of disorder is constant, stayed only by strong monarchs who contain their adversaries. Whether viewed on the level of society or in the realm of man's spirit, the confrontation with disorder looms as a permanent vocation. On both levels the final destiny is soteriological; it is ultimate freedom. The stabilizing of order by the king and the exorcism of the demonic by religious incantation[43] are both requisite to the ultimate goal of Nibbana. The establishment of the sacred boundaries (*sīmā*) of the Sangha as coterminous with the sacred city of Anuradhapura by Mahinda Thera and King Devanampiyatissa symbolizes the inclusion of social and political order within the larger order of the Dhamma, which is the source of freedom from disorder itself. The symbiotic ideal which this suggests is seen to have repercussions which incorporate not only society, but all nature and the cosmos at large. It is in this perspective that one can comprehend the urgency to maintain both the purity of the doctrine and the unity of the Sangha. With the continuum between the "secular" and the "sacred" so conceived, any threat to order in the latter was automatically construed as disruptive of the former. It is to the politically relevant dimensions of Dhamma that we must now turn.

III. THE MONARCHY-SANGHA RELATIONSHIP

In the long history of Sinhalese Buddhism there is no relationship more complex or more crucial than that existing between the monarchy and the Sangha. Of all the pithy sayings concluding each chapter of the *Mahāvaṃsa* none perhaps is more telling in this respect than the following: "Thus, reflecting that sovereignty, being the source of manifold works of merit, is at the same time the source of many an injustice, a man of pious heart will never enjoy it as if it were sweet food mixed with poison."[44] The Sangha's historic dependence upon the monarchy for support, protection, and confirmation of the faith has not been an unmixed blessing. At the core of the issue is the understanding of Dhamma and the role each institution had in its furtherance. Not unrelated are the problems caused by a religion's becoming established, problems which can be devastating for the religion as for the society in general, raising the very question of what the "establishment" of Buddhism (or of any religious faith) means. The most extreme instance of fanatical religious and national sentiment oc-

---

[43] According to Adikaram, the recitation of the *Parittas* (*Protection Suttas*) in Ceylon dates back at least to the late fourth century A. D., though they are part of the Pali Canon itself. They are still used extensively, now primarily in exorcism rites. Originally, they had a public import and were chanted in times of famine, plague, or other ill. Cf. Adikaram, *op. cit.*, pp. 143-144.

[44] *Mahāvaṃsa*, p. 266.

curring in Sinhalese history was in the kingship of its classical hero, Dutthaga-mani, who, after the pattern of Asoka, lamented the carnage his victories had wrought.[45] While similar in outward form, the resemblance to Asoka stops there. In the vanguard of a crusade, Dutthagamani, with a relic in his spear and accompanied by five hundred bhikkhus, marches into battle with the Tamils, declaring solemnly: "Not for the joy of sovereignty is this toil of mine, my striving (has been) ever to establish the doctrine of the Sambuddha."[46] And even his remorse following the slaughter is short-lived, for the Sangha knowing his thoughts send eight arahants to comfort him: "From this deed arises no hindrance in thy way to heaven. Only one and a half human beings have been slain here by thee, O lord of men. . . . Unbelievers and men of evil life were the rest, not more to be esteemed than beasts. But as for thee, thou wilt bring glory to the doctrine of the Buddha in manifold ways; therefore cast away care from thy heart." "Thus exhorted by them the great king took comfort."[47]

The very inclusion of this passage in the chronicles of Ceylon, while ironic, is of immense import. While neither monarch nor Sangha in this guise could be a model, the tradition's refusal to gloss over murder and self-justification be-comes instructive for history. As the conscience of the nation, the Sangha, so-bered by unending warfare and intrigue, is recording its alarm. Though different stylistically from the Hebrew prophets, one detects a comparable judgment, upon themselves as upon those directly responsible. Again and again, the bhikkhu community through these chronicles records its own need for purification, along-side that of the nation. Part of the solemn charge given to the king is that of helping to maintain a strong and united Order. "It was his right to see that the religion was kept pure [*sodhesi sāsanam*] and in its pristine condition. Conse-crated in the ceremonial of the *abhiseka* or 'anointing' with rites at which in time the *Sangha* assisted, the king was head of the state with power to purify the *sāsana*, as he often did."[48] The monarch, in turn, was kept responsible by the Sangha, his meritorious works duly registered in the royal annals, his violations no less noted.[49] That there was friction between them one would expect, but that the ideal of reciprocity endured cannot be questioned. In essence, it was a symbiosis rooted in tradition and having consequences for what it meant to be a Buddhist community in the best sense of the word, a *sāvaka-sangha* or ideal social order.

As in every other way, the prototype for this relationship may be found in

---

[45] *Ibid.*, p. 177. "Sitting then on the terrace of the royal palace, adorned, lighted with fragrant lamps and filled with many a perfume, magnificent with nymphs in the guise of dancing-girls, while he rested on his soft and fair couch, covered with costly draperies, he, looking back upon his victory, great though it was, knew no joy, remem-bering that thereby was wrought the destruction of millions (of beings)."

[46] *Ibid.*, p. 171.

[47] *Ibid.*, p. 178. Regarding the one and a half: "The one had come unto the (three) refuges, the other had taken on himself the five precepts."

[48] Ludowyk, *op. cit.*, p. 101.

[49] Geiger, *op. cit.*, p. 204.

the Buddha's life, here his reported associations with monarchs. The sovereignty of political power is subsumed under the sovereignty of the Dhamma in the *Dīpavaṃsa* account of King Bimbisara's vision at the age of eight: "A Khattiya is in need of sovereignty; he, the Enlightened one, the bull among men, should arise in my kingdom; the Tathāgata should approach to show himself first to me, he should preach the everlasting norm, I should penetrate (into) the excellent (norm)."[50] Tradition cements the fealty of king to Dhamma in the very appealing story of Asoka's attraction to and conversion by the young bhikkhu Nigrodha. Searching for "truth and untruth," "for the virtuous and skilful," Asoka tests person after person in vain and in discouragement asks: "When should I approach to have a sight of good men? Listening to this good saying I shall give my sovereignty along with the kingdom."[51] At one point he sees Nigrodha and addresses an aide: "Behold, quickly conduct that monk, the young man moving on the road like an elephant, graceful and peaceful by nature, fearless and possessed of the quality of tranquility."[52] Nigrodha is brought in and, "like the fearless king of gods, Sakka," mounts the imperial throne, to Asoka's amazement and delight. The king then utters the word which depicts the Sangha's vocation to monarch and people alike: "Teach me the Norm which you have learnt. You will be my teacher and I shall be taught by you. Oh great sage, I will act according to your word. Instruct me, I will listen to your instruction."[53] The monk speaks; the king listens; and the teachings of the Buddha come alive. Asoka then takes refuge in the three gems, bestowing upon the bhikkhu community his loyalty and his larder, saying, "as much as the monks desire I give them whatever they choose."[54]

What follows becomes the model of royal patronage to the Sangha in recognition of the Dhamma's true majesty. The monks' needs are met; viharas without number are built; and in the Third Council the true Dhamma is compiled and preserved. One further test put to Asoka in answer to his question "Whose generosity toward the doctrine of the Blessed One was ever (so) great (as

---

[50] *Dīpavaṃsa*, p. 151.

[51] *Ibid.*, pp. 172-173.

[52] *Ibid.*, p. 174.

[53] *Ibid.*, p. 175. The *Mahāvaṃsa* likewise describes this scene and adds an account of how the paths of these two had crossed in an earlier life, confirming the destined nature of their meeting and of Nigrodha's preeminence. Cf. *Mahāvaṃsa*, pp. 29-32.

[54] *Dīpavaṃsa*, p. 178. The story of royal support for the economic needs of the Sangha has been told by many; Geiger's book referred to above is one example. Through the tax structure, through land grants, through sizeable endowments, among other measures, the Order received considerable fiscal assistance. Grants made to the bhikkhu community were known as *saṅgha-bhoga*. There also grew up the practice that whatever was produced in certain locales was for the *vihāra*, a practice known as *lābha-sīmā*, related as it was to the whole concept of *sīma*, where the boundaries of the Sangha are coextensive with the boundaries of the state. This kind of economic, social and political power granted to the Order made it in time influential in the making of policy. It was a secular force which no king could ignore, let alone a moral power of substance. Cf. Arasaratnam, *op. cit.*, pp. 75-76, 80-81.

mine)?" shows even more the king's responsibility toward the Sangha and seals the eventual tie with Lanka. When told there was no one more generous than he, Asoka presses his luck and asks, "Is there a kinsman of Buddha's religion like unto me?" The reply of Moggaliputta Thera has implications not only for Asoka and succeeding monarchs, but for all people: "[Only] he who lets son or daughter enter the religious order is a kinsman of the religion and withal a giver of gifts."[55]

A great deal more could be said about the king's protection and support of the Sangha. The chronicles are replete with accounts of royal patronage to both Sangha and society; they are no less specific about lack of patronage as well.[56] Ideally, too, the ruler was expected to be the *fidei defensor*, protecting the Dhamma from heretical incursions, settling disputes among the bhikkhus, encouraging the teaching and spread of the doctrine. In actuality, kings were seen to support now one vihara, now another, promoting "orthodoxy" at certain points in history, "heretical sects" at others. As with the misuse of power in general, the chronicles are candid about the infidelity of certain kings who fell into the clutches of wayward and lawless monks. One must always remember, however, that the story is being told from the Mahavihara point of view. In any case, our concern here is for the image of ideal reciprocity. On this score, the picture is unambiguous; it is a division of labor with both parties dedicated to the same goal. This is seen in the frequent offering of the kingdom to the sasana by the monarch, symbolizing his own recognition of the state's purpose. While always returned to him, it was a gesture of acknowledgement that his authority is both delegated and responsible.[57] The division of labor is seen also in the fact that, while it was the king's right and duty to insure that the doctrine be taught, it was in fact the Sangha's task to provide the instruction. The most poignant example of this may be noted in Dutthagamani's attempt to propagate the faith himself. "He seated himself in the preacher's chair in the centre of the spacious hall and made ready to give the august assembly a discourse on some religious topic from the *Mangala-Sutta*. But, although he was quite familiar with the Sacred Scriptures, he could not proceed; he descended from the pulpit 'perspiring profusely'; he had realized how difficult was the task of the teachers, and his munificence towards them was made greater."[58]

---

[55] *Mahāvaṃsa*, pp. 42-43. The immediate son and daughter in question were, of course, Mahinda and Samghamitta who received the *pabbajjā* or ordination into the Order, but by extension the same criterion of kinsmanship applies to all parents.

[56] Section four on the Ideal King will sketch further aspects of the monarch's role as patron.

[57] Cf. Rahula, *op cit.*, p. 75. The antiphonal nature of the oblation is caught in the *Mahāvaṃsa* description of Moggallana's ascent to the throne: "He approached the community, greeted it respectfully and pleased with this community, he as a mark of distinction, presented it with his umbrella. The community returned it to him." Cf. p. 46. The white parasol or umbrella (*seta chatta*) was traditionally the prime symbol of royal authority.

[58] Malalasekere, *op. cit.*, p. 38.

It would be a serious mistake, on the other hand, to view the monarch's relationship to the Sangha independently of his relationship to society and the body politic as a whole. It would be more true to say that the ideal of symbiosis between thera and king was symbolic of the ideal reciprocity between all persons in the society. As the monarch can be portrayed as Cakkavatti at one end of the spectrum and Everyman at the other, so he can be in search of the Dhamma's meaning at the same time that he is its protector. It is this dual portrayal of each king which, as in the case of Asoka, commends him as an illustration of each person's striving toward "greater merit" in the short run and Nibbana ultimately. The concept of reciprocity is paramount to the Buddhist notion of an ideal society. This is beautifully conceived in the *Sigālovāda Sutta*, sometimes regarded as the "Whole Duty" or *Vinaya* of the Buddhist layman. In it are depicted the ideal relationships between people in various roles or circumstances (e.g., husband-wife, parents-children, employers-servants, etc.). Though deceptively simple in presentation, it is a part of the Pali Canon which has exercised immense influence because it somehow catches the rhythm of what authentic association is all about. We shall explore this further in the final section. At this point let us examine the king's socio-political task in helping to make this reciprocity possible. It is in this regard that the idea of Dhamma has decidedly relevant social implications. This was put succinctly in the following statement:

> The early Buddhist philosophy of kingship is a compound of three distinct attitudes. Although the early Buddhists betray feelings of disquiet, bordering on fear, about the nature and functions of kingship as it existed in their times, they see no alternative to it and declare it to be absolutely essential to prevent humanity from lapsing into a state of anarchy. Finally, confronted with the fact of kingship and the absolute necessity for it for orderly human existence, they attempt to tame absolute political power by infusing into it a spirit of higher morality.[59]

Such a statement could have been affirmed either by Asoka or the Sinhalese chroniclers as the essence of the political task under Dhamma. The same ambivalence toward worldly power, the same acceptance of its inevitability, the same striving to make it responsible are as evident throughout Buddhist history as in its early days. The frequent assumptions by Westerners that Theravada, especially, lacks a social ethic cannot be maintained in the light of overwhelming evidence to the contrary. As with all social philosophy we are here talking about an ideal, but it must also be viewed as an ideal which had policy repercussions. Again, the prime, but by no means only, example is that of Asoka. If Asoka provided the norm, it was one emulated in countless versions within Sinhalese, Burmese, and Thai history. In these and other cultural contexts can be seen a repeated clash of historic cruelty with the Asokan ideal. This should surprise no one; the chronicles themselves document this, reign after reign. Were this not

[59] B. G. Gokhale, "Early Buddhist Kingship," *The Journal of Asian Studies,* Vol. XXVI, No. 1, p. 15.

so, the Dhamma would be fulfilled, not only preached. The carnage which brought Asoka's conscience into sensitivity was but a ripple in the world's history of slaughter, but the paradigm which his response provided continued to effect Buddhist communities. It was finally this which became the model and norm, not the political ideals of Kautalya.[60] In essence, this was to assert that the state is not an end in itself, but a means toward a higher end of which it is the servant. This is always the more difficult task than that of absolutism, for the higher end is always partially obscure and is never permanently reached within the political order.

It was this realistic humility, this acceptance of the lesser but crucial task of creating a just order, which constitutes the crux of the Buddhist ideal of kingship at its best. Acknowledgement of the limitations of its role makes the monarchy's reciprocity with the Sangha a viable one. The purpose of one was to create and maintain an ordered society within which men can pursue freely the greater goal beyond order. The purpose of the other was to discover this greater goal for themselves and to show all men the path to it. These two purposes were not at odds, only in tension. Order precedes liberation; liberation requires order. Besides, the type of order envisaged was one in which all men's basic needs were met; it was order at the heart of which was justice. It was the latter which prompted Asoka and later Buddhists to dig wells, provide rest houses, construct tanks, have mercy on animals, feed the poor and a host of other manifestations. But it was his reason for taking these and other steps which reveals the Buddhist character of his concerns. "These are trifling comforts," he says. "For the people have received various facilities from previous kings as well as from me. But I have done what I have primarily in order that the people may follow the path of Dharma with faith and devotion."[61]

It was both the motive for his actions and the awareness that Nibbana cannot be pursued when people's needs are ignored which made his political ethic a new entry into history. It created in the process a Buddhist ethos sometimes called *lokka-nibbāna* (or Nibbana in this world), which is a confusing term when what it really connotes is the compatibility, even interdependence, between social concern on the one hand and the quest for tranquility (*upekkhā*) on the other. Far from being indifference to the world, it is only through upekkha that genuine concern arises. Coupled with this was the very pragmatic realization that the pursuit of Nibbana necessitates leisured meditation and that this requires both economic sufficiency and a stable socio-political order.[62] The king's task, therefore, was to stabilize the natural and social order, not "change" society so much as "stabilize" it. The odyssey of the human spirit was viewed within a

[60] *Ibid.*, 21.

[61] Nikam and McKeon, *op. cit.*, p. 64. Joseph M. Kitagawa has put it this way: "Asoka found in the Dharma a Universal principle, applicable both to religious and secular domains, as well as to all men, Buddhist and non-Buddhist alike." Cf. his article entitled "Buddhism and Asian Politics," *Asian Survey*, Vol. II, No. 5, p. 2.

[62] Sarkisyanz, *op. cit.*, p. 56.

cosmological and historical pattern where there is no progress, only order and disorder, both relative, both filled with potential. Authentic progress comes only to the inner man; it is achieved by each man anew, moments building upon moments, each man, as the chronicles put it, going "according to his *kamma*" (*yathākammaṃ*). Over this no state, nor established religion, holds sway. It acts only as prelude, to facilitate or to obstruct. Like all worldly sovereignty, it is "sweet food mixed with poison."

IV. SOCIETY-COSMOS RELATIONSHIP

The Asokan concept of Dharma-vijaya (conquest through righteousness) pertained, in his thinking, not only to the present age but to the enduring future. If this eschatological note was not developed until later centuries, it was clearly struck in the emperor's hopes that his newly established pattern of conquest would become normative. One clue to this lies in his words that "whatever effort King Priyadarśī makes is for the sake of the life hereafter and in order that men may be saved from enslavement."[63] Like the chronicles of Ceylon the *Edicts* of Asoka betray no illusion about the difficulty of the task, a task which "rich and poor alike will find . . . difficult to do . . . unless they make a great effort and renounce all other aims."[64] It remains for this final section to look at the eschatological dimensions of Dharma-vijaya, to see how it came increasingly over time to be united with certain cosmological assumptions about the nature of reality, certain emerging visions of the Ideal King, and certain growing expectations about the City of Righteousness.

While it is risky trying to date the emergence of these ideas, it is equally true that they were prominent in the time of the *Mahāvaṃsa* and that, in relatively undeveloped form, they can be found in the Pali Canon. Tradition, indeed, ascribes them to the time of the Buddha himself, with the insistence by Mahayana that they represent the core of his teaching. Without stopping to argue these points, it is pertinent to this essay to observe their manifestation within the Sinhalese chronicles, especially within the *Mahāvaṃsa*, for upon these concepts depend the most profound ingredients of an ideal social order as perceived by Theravada Buddhists. To reflect upon their meaning within this context affords a clearer understanding not only of what Buddhism construes by Dhamma but of the relationship between the three gems in which Buddhists have taken refuge.

1. The first of these concepts to be explored here stems from the sustained conviction within the Buddhist community about the essential oneness or interrelatedness of reality, a concept having both temporal and spatial dimensions.[65] The most seminal idea at this point is that of *paṭicca-samuppāda*, a notion central

---

[63] Nikam and McKeon, *op. cit.*, p. 48.

[64] *Ibid.*

[65] It goes without saying that these convictions are not developed "conceptually" either within the chronicles or within ancient Buddhist tradition. It is true, nonetheless, that the raw material for them may be found throughout the writings.

to all Buddhism which has been translated in various ways, though most frequently as "dependent origination." Basically, it suggests that, while there is no *original* causative agent or event, all reality is a network of causes and effects, producing various degrees of good and evil, order and disorder, and within it men can discover through discipline and eventually enlightenment the ability to cause or bring about their own liberation. In personal terms, it conveys the conviction that each man can come to realize the essential non-duality of "self" and "others," the fundamental union of all life, and the folly of clinging (*taṇhā*) to the self-defeating notions of "me" and "mine" (*anatta*). Fundamental to this realization is his awakening to the fact of impermanence (*anicca*) and his own capacity not simply to live tranquilly within it but to embody joy, harmony and compassion. In social terms, it conveys the sense in which the actions, words, and desires of each person fit into a framework of inter-relationship whereby what one does affects all. And, in cosmic terms, it conveys the more immense awareness that the entire universe is a fabric with parts dependent upon each other, a tissue of entities making up one whole.[66] It is intrinsic to Buddhist social concern that authentic community comes only through the unfolding consciousness of persons that their identity cannot be known apart from others. The most basic term for compassion, *karuṇā*, suggests a widening self-identification with all that lives.[67]

While this notion is common to all Buddhist testimony, its configurations in the Sinhalese chronicles are vivid, engaging, and unique. One could do an entire study of the *Mahāvaṃsa* focussing on the personal, social and cosmic aspects of paticca-samuppada, as they are manifold. Each chapter makes an assessment of the whys and wherefores of circumstances and events, interpreting them in the light of actions taken or ignored, tracing the destinies of kings, in particular, "according to their *kamma*." We shall focus here on the sense of cosmic consciousness which the chroniclers portray as they weave together the events of history with tradition's interpretation.

As might be expected, one finds the delineation of cosmic awareness peculiarly expressive in the accounts of royal consecrations, for at times like these relationships are made most explicit: those of monarch and Sangha and people to each other, those of time past to time present to time future, those of this place to all places. This is true with the kingly prototype, Asoka. "Straightway after his consecration his command spread so far as a yojana (upward) into the air and downward into the (depth of the) earth."[68] "The sense of this passage, not rightly understood up to the present time," Wilhelm Geiger quaintly suggests in a footnote, "is evidently this: not only men upon the earth but also

[66] Cf. Edward Conze's essay "Dharma as a Spiritual, Social and Cosmic Force" in Paul Kuntz, ed., *The Concept of Order* (Seattle: University of Washington, 1967), pp. 239-252, in which he sees the same tripodic nature of the Buddhist orientation but develops it in a different direction.

[67] Sarkisyanz, *op. cit.*, p. 41.

[68] *Mahāvaṃsa*, p. 28.

the spirits of the air and the earth heard and obeyed Asoka's command."[69] Following this more general statement, the chronicle elaborates the organic harmony which comprised Asoka's rule:

> From the Himalaya did the devas bring for cleansing the teeth twigs of nāga-creeper. . . . The spirits of the air brought garments of five colours. . . . Out of the nāga-kingdom the nāgas (brought) stuff, coloured like the jasmine-blossom and without a seam . . .; parrots brought daily . . . waggon-loads of rice. Mice converted this rice, unbroken, into grains without husk or powder. . . . Perpetually did honey-bees prepare honey for him. . . . Karavīka-birds, graceful and sweet of voice, came and made delightful music for the king.[70]

Reference was made earlier to what happened at Devanampiyatissa's consecration, as a result of his merit: "In the whole isle of Laṅkā treasures and jewels that had been buried deep rose to the surface of the earth."[71] The most tumultuous display of rhythmic harmony, uniting man and beast, is found in the depiction of the consecration festival of Parakkamabahu, the Great, in 1154 A.D.[72] While more tailored to the local setting, it is no less cosmic in orientation.

All of these instances carry the conviction that the monarch's role in relationship to society and cosmos is to sustain the living harmony underlying all existence. Royal power is the instrument of cosmic power. As with the classic Chinese understanding of the emperor as the "Son of Heaven," the character of whose rule effected not only society but nature, so here one finds the assumed correspondence between an evil monarch and disasters in nature, or between goodness and harmony. The assumption throughout the *Mahāvaṃsa* is how much men of power can do, providing they have good understanding.[73] Sovereignty, when purged of poison, causes works which are sweet. Present in this view are both a "high" and a "low" estimate of royal power, estimates which are cautious, yet hopeful, at the same time. It is essentially a view of human nature which is realistic yet supremely sensitive to man's potential. Above all, it stands awed before the power of the Dhamma. In commenting upon Elara, the Tamil, who for forty-five years ruled justly over Lanka, the chronicler speculates, if a non-believer can be so good, how much more a believer![74]

It is again at this point that one sees the impact of the Sangha's relationship to the monarchy and why the latter remained pledged to the welfare of the Order. The ideal symbiosis between these institutions was the primal instance, the archetype, of what personal, social, and cosmic symbiosis involved. As an ideal, approximated in reality or not, it was the model of what all reciprocity entailed. When the Dhamma was protected, the monarchy thrived, the Sangha

[69] *Ibid.*
[70] *Ibid.*
[71] *Ibid.*, pp. 77-78.
[72] *Cūlavaṃsa*, I, pp. 347-348.
[73] *Mahāvaṃsa*, p. 245.
[74] *Ibid.*, p. 145.

became a blessing, and the people flourished. Any break in the continuum and disorder prevailed. The most symbolic presentation of this in the chronicles may be that chapter in the *Mahāvaṃsa* entitled "The Acceptance of the Mahavihara" in which Mahinda marks off locations in Anuradhapura, the sacred city, on which various buildings of the Great Vihara will be constructed in future years. At each announcement there is a quaking of the earth. As with the account of the building of the Mahathupa later under Dutthagamani, the tradition is making clear the connection between heaven and earth, between the present moment and all moments, between the sacrality of the Dhamma and all else. Ironically, the establishing of the boundaries (sima) is the removal of all boundaries. It is man's way of saying that in order to see continuity, to experience reciprocity, one must establish distinctions where in reality none exist. The planting of the Bodhi-tree and the bringing of the relics are ways of making visible, therefore present, what was never absent, though always invisible. At two points in the chronicles, both in relationship to the arrival or enshrining of relics, the same words are used: "Thus are the Buddhas incomprehensible, and incomprehensible is the nature of the Buddhas, and incomprehensible is the reward of those who have faith in the incomprehensible."[75]

It is in such a vein that any would have the audacity to claim that *saṃsāra* is *Nirvāṇa*,[76] for it is through the attaining of enlightenment that samsara's full potential may be imagined, a potential which otherwise remains obscure because of the enslavement it more obviously reflects. It is faith in the very incomprehensibility of the transformation of ignorance into wisdom, of self-preoccupation into compassion for others, which is expressed devotionally within the chronicles. The import behind the profusion of festivals which color the pages of these documents and the lives of Sinhalese Buddhists is clearly this: they stand for hearts gladdened by the miracle of release from bondage. Were their awareness of fear, bitterness and intransigency not so vivid, they would be less expressive of joy and wonder. This too explains in part the seeming preoccupation with stupa-building, image-making and celebration in general. It was a community mindful of blessings received, so that to adorn is to be adoring, to bestow gifts is to acknowledge the worth-ship of what has been received. In the words of the *Mahāvaṃsa*: "Commanded by the lord of men, they, filled with deep reverence for the Sage (Buddha), adorned the place in manifold ways."[77] It was a community having received a foretaste of what was possible for all men, of what society could become, and of what cosmic harmony would entail. The tension between the promise of a reconciled universe and the experience of a world in suffering made each more vivid. If the age of the Buddha (*Buddhavassa*) had begun, its consummation occurred only in the imagination. The Wheel of the Law had been turned, but Dharma-vijaya's fulfillment remained alive only in expectation.

---

[75] *Ibid.*, pp. 120, 219.
[76] Admittedly, a Mahayana claim, but made in other ways by Theravada.
[77] *Ibid.*, p. 192. Cf. also, p. 242.

2. Of one piece with this vision of unity and this continued experiencing of distress and enmity was the unfolding anticipation of an Ideal King, a monarch whose rule by righteousness would occasion and cement the reality of the universe's intrinsic oneness. At the heart of any apocalyptic vision is the awareness of a soteriological necessity. To the tradition's poignant sensitivity to mankind's suffering was added the gradual acknowledgement of the king's role as *bodhisatta* (Sanskrit, *bodhisattva*) and of the appearance in new guise of the Cakkavatti figure. Unquestionably, this development reflects the influence of Mahayana sects upon Sinhalese consciousness, but it unfolded in ways which did no violence to the orthodox insistence that man was the agent of his own release. This point has not yet been stressed enough in discussions of the interplay between the two major paths within Buddhist tradition. It is in part the intent of this section to highlight the compatibility of "taking refuge in oneself" with "taking refuge in Buddha, Dhamma and Sangha," both of which are essential to Buddhist soteriological understanding.

Many scholars have traced the appearance and increasing effect of the bodhisatta concept in India, Ceylon, and elsewhere. It is the task here to perceive its emergence within the Sinhalese chronicles, for the part it plays in Theravada generally without question stems from these developments, influenced by Indian concepts as they were. While one can read back into discussions of earlier reigns the same intent, the earliest explicit reference in the chronicles to the bodhisatta-like nature of any monarch is to Buddhadasa who ruled in the late fourth century A.D. The reference here, to be sure, is almost in passing, but it is unmistakable: "The Ruler lived openly before the people the life that bodhisattas lead and had pity for (all) beings as a father (has pity for) his children."[78] The significance of this comment can be minimized as a mere figure of speech and as one which may be found earlier in the Pali Canon itself. It is, however, in the impression one gets of the nature and character of Buddhadasa, who "shone like the Perfectly Enlightened One," and of his reign that one detects the beginning of a new phenomenon, a savior-king, one whose meritorious action heals the sick, woos men out of enmity, and creates happiness for all his subjects.[79] Even earlier, in the person of Sirisamghabodhi in the early fourth century, we are put in the presence of one who, though not called a bodhisatta in the account, makes a self-oblation of his life that his realm may be freed from famine and drought.[80]

It is possible to discover at least four elements in the chronicler's judgment of what constituted a righteous monarch which contributed to, or were a part of, the emerging Cakkavatti image. The *first* relates to the qualities such a king should (does) possess. While these may be found attributed to many rulers in various ways, the most succinct attributions are to Buddhadasa and to his eldest son, Upatissa. "Endowed with the ten qualities of kings (*dasa rājadhammā*), while avoiding the four wrong paths, practising justice, [Buddhadāsa] won over

[78] *Cūlavamsa*, I, p. 10.
[79] *Ibid.*, pp. 9-17.
[80] *Mahāvamsa*, pp. 261-263.

his subjects by the four heart-winning qualities (*cattāri saṃgahavatthūni.*) "[81] Even more was ascribed to the son: "Shunning the ten sinful actions, he practised the ten meritorious works (*puññakiriyā*); the King fulfilled the ten royal duties and the ten *pāramitās*. By the four heart-winning qualities he won over the four regions of the world."[82] Geiger's footnotes detail these qualities, though, of course, these were familiar to all readers in ancient Lanka, indeed, to all bhikkhus and upasakas, let alone to each monarch. The very cataloguing of the qualities was intended as a focus for meditation even more than as a description of certain kings. But there can be no questioning the lofty concept of kingship which these revealed.

The *second* element, present throughout the portrayal of a righteous ruler, is one to which we have referred before, namely, his role as patron and supporter to the Sangha. This need not be elaborated here except to say that one finds more explicit reference to social welfare measures appearing in the fourth and fifth centuries, and beyond, than earlier. The giving of alms, the concern for wages, the digging of wells, the planting of trees, and especially the construction of tanks and canals are of frequent mention. While all these obviously occurred before, the very increased mention says much about the king's function as not only an establisher of order but as a creator and maintainer of a just and thriving society, which was held to be an intrinsic part of the ideal. The most graphic figure of the monarch at this point is one assigned to Udaya II, who was "like to a wishing tree, a dispenser of blessings for all the needy," an image often used in Indian mythology to depict the bounty of heaven.[83] This corroborates Geiger's comment that "the greatest virtue of a king was considered to be charitableness" (*mahākaruṇā*), a quality stemming from identification with one's subjects, not simply from feelings of kindness.[84]

Thirdly, the ideal monarch is held to be a paragon of what it means to be a man, not just a patron of society or Sangha. As the king takes on Cakkavatti proportions, with all its soteriological connotations, this depiction of him as a paragon for all men becomes increasingly important. There are a number of kings in the chronicles who are portrayed in this fashion, but two are especially intriguing, for different reasons: one (Sena II) seems almost the epitome of perfection and is therefore somewhat abstract, albeit no less a model of manhood; the other (Aggabodhi VIII) is portrayed in very concrete and human terms, albeit no less an image of perfection. To juxtapose comments about these persons helps create the impression of the tension, yet continuity, between the ideal as it was imagined and the reality which sometimes took flesh. "Showing conduct like that of the kings of the first age of the world, pious, wealthy, heroic, generous, impartial, succouring the needy . . . [Sena] represented in his spotless fame and his splendid ability, as it were, a union of the sun and the moon:

[81] *Cūlavaṃsa*, I, p. 10.
[82] *Ibid.*, p. 17.
[83] *Ibid.*, p. 159.
[84] Geiger, *op. cit.*, p. 133.

richly gifted with unblemished qualities, practising every kind of virtue, devoid
of all sin, weary of the cycle of births, his gaze fixed on the highest."[85] This
statement is replete with connotations, religious and political, which might profitably be explored. Suffice it to say here that there could hardly be a more un-
stinted accolade of what Buddhist manhood should comprise than this. While
beyond the reach of the ordinary layman, to be sure, it would at least constitute
his understanding of the upasaka vocation as well as engender in him a sense of
the ideal king's paradigmatic nature.

Side by side with this may be put the portrayal of Aggabodhi VIII with
whom identification may be more possible but who, nevertheless, embodies traits
no less uncommon:

> The King found pleasure in the serving of his mother day and night. He went
> to wait on her already early in the morning, rubbed her head with oil, perfumed
> the parts moist with sweat, cleaned her nails and bathed her carefully. He clad
> her himself in a new garment, pleasant to the touch, and the castoff raiment he
> took and cleaned it himself. . . . After making obeisance before her three times,
> and walking, with right side facing, round her . . . he offered her delicious food
> with his own hand. . . . [Then] when he had put in order her chamber, fragrant
> with sweet odours, he carefully prepared there with his own hand her couch,
> washed her feet, rubbed her gently with fragrant oil, sat by her rubbing her
> limbs and sought to make her sleep. . . . Then happy at his action, and ever
> thinking of her, he went home. As long as she lived he served her in this way.[86]

The inclusion of this passage in the chronicles is hardly for reader interest alone.
It bespeaks not only of true filial respect but of the essence of bodhisatta-like
tenderness, the sort of reciprocity counselled in the *Sigālovāda Sutta*, of which we
have spoken before. It is one, too, with the sense of fittingness which sees and
responds to the needs of all creation. As was said about one king: "For the
bhikkhu community, for the laity, for fishes, game and birds, for his kinsfolk and
for the troops he did everything that was mete for them."[87] Lastly, it is one with
the adoration and reverence shown toward the Buddha by pious followers, in
token of blessings received. It is at the core of purity, which manifests itself in
compassion, service, and self-oblation.

The *fourth* and crowning attribute of the ideal king is the catalytic effect his
meritorious actions have upon other people. We are dealing here not simply
with a paragon whose qualities are worthy of emulation but with a charisma and
power which call into existence traits dormant and unrealized in the lives of
others. It is in this respect that the soteriological efficacy of the Cakkavatti takes
on a dimension present but untapped in earlier tradition. As is true about the
chronicler's judgment both of power and of human nature, the charisma of the
ruler has demonic possibilities as well as beneficent, "for it is the rule with
living creatures: what he who is master does, evil or good, the same is done by
his subjects; let the wise man take heed of that."[88] The lesson of history, as

[85] *Cūlavaṃsa*, I, p. 147.
[86] *Ibid.*, pp. 132-133.
[87] *Ibid.*, p. 119.
[88] *Ibid.*, p. 100.

recorded in these pages, makes clear the double-edged nature of the monarch's effect. But, in the same breath in which he cites this warning, he comments about the royal influence for good: "Thus he was in all his dealings one to whom the teaching of the Buddha was the highest (good), and vying with him all the people also fulfilled the (commands of that) doctrine."[89] About another king, he writes: "Everyone in his kingdom cultivated action which leads to Heaven, for as the monarch acts so do also his subjects."[90] Finally, about Dutthagamani, whose own struggle with impurity and whose later meritorious actions are both seen as classic, the *Mahāvaṃsa* says: "Thus do the pious themselves perform pure deeds of merit, in order to obtain the most glorious of all blessings; and they, with a pure heart, make also others to perform them in order to win a following of eminent people of many kinds."[91]

In all these instances the basic assumption is made: like king, like subjects. It is possible to find plausible historic factors which influenced this development. Paul Mus has suggested that "the charismatic figure of the Wheel-wielding King (*cakravartin*) grew in size and was credited with increasing soteriological powers, as a compensation for and prospective help against too positive and immediate woes."[92] Walpola Rahula has pointed out its relationship to religionationalism, saying that "by about the 10th century, this belief had become so strong that the king of Ceylon had not only to be a Buddhist but also a Bodhisattva."[93] Undoubtedly, too, there were often quasi-magical elements present which trivialized and jeopardized the more profound implications. Without question, in the hands of some, the soteriological conception of the king was little more than a clever rationalization for state power. The validity of these and other explanations are pertinent and valuable, but they do not exhaust the internal meaning of the phenomenon and its relevance to the social order.

In essence, what one sees unfolding over many centuries, influenced both by the Sanskritic notion of kingship and by Mahayana ideas about the bodhisattva, was a merging of two distinct but overlapping notions of sovereignty: one, of the socio-political order; the other, of the cosmos at large. Paradoxically, the original choice of vocations which was put before the infant Siddhattha is now revealed as false dichotomy, for as the Universal Ruler or Ideal King is also the Cakkavatti or Bodhisatta, so the Buddha is the supreme monarch, the master of heaven and earth. Whether viewed personally or cosmically, only one who rules himself is fit to rule others and he who teaches men Dharma-vijaya or conquest

---

[89] *Ibid.*, p. 99.

[90] *Ibid.*, p. 111. He continues: "Therefore should a wise king ever practice piety; in every place where men dwell he will become renowned and finally, surrounded by his companions, he enters Nirvana." In a footnote Geiger suggests the pragmatic advantages to a king to educate his people to piety, as it insures order in the realm. No doubt there were monarchs who practiced piety for just this reason, as well as those whose practice was otherwise motivated.

[91] *Mahāvaṃsa*, p. 219.

[92] Paul Mus, Preface to *Buddhist Backgrounds of the Burmese Revolution*, p. xviii.

[93] Rahula, *op. cit.*, p. 62.

through righteousness is the ruler of all. In evidence is a kind of parabolic movement, which has obvious liturgical ramifications, from king to Bodhisatta King (Buddha) back to king again; an offering of self to one who taught release from self so that one may serve others with justice, compassion and tranquility. As Sarkisyanz points out in quoting from the *Kāka-Jātaka*, "a king laid his kingdom at the Bodhisattva's feet, but the Bodhisattva restored it to the king . . . beseeching him to shield all living creatures from harm."[94] One is struck by the identical symbolism here with that practiced by Sinhalese monarchs, as they offered their kingdom to the Sangha as vice-regent for the Buddha, or, in one case, to the newly arrived relics as the very presence of Gotama himself.

The explicit connection with the Buddha is, of course, central to the whole conception. Here too one can perceive a parabola-like movement, as, for instance, in the *Mahā-Sudassana Sutta* where the Buddha reveals himself to Ananda as having been in another life the Great King of Glory. It is important to keep in mind that the only bodhisatta recognized by Theravada is the Buddha (or Bodhisatta) Metteyya, the Buddha-to-come. The expectations of his coming have played a major role in the social and political ethos of Theravada communities.[95] The aspirations of kings in both Ceylon and Burma were to become the Bodhisatta Metteya in their next life. "Not only renovation but also fulfillment of Buddhism was expected from Mettaya: universal compassion is to become through him a cosmic reality."[96] In this conviction we have a blending of the three ideas mentioned at the start of this section, namely, a conviction regarding the essential oneness of reality, a vision about the role of the Ideal King, and an expectation of the forthcoming City of Righteousness. In the various titles used for the Ideal King[97] it was manifest that in him was embodied a syzygy or genuine symbiosis by means of which, because the two wheels of the temporal and spiritual domains[98] were harmonized, there would emerge a harmonizing of heaven and earth, man and nature, king and people, society as a whole, and man with himself. The image of the Golden Age in the past was projected into the future as a time when all the ills of the present age would be cured and its antinomies reconciled. In the meantime, despite the strength of the expectation, there endured the awareness that we are living "between the times," in an age of decline between what once was and what in time will be. The vision of what will be is focused in the concept of a City of Righteousness.

3. Akin to the notion of an Ideal King, the City of Righteousness may be seen by the mind's eye alone. As the presence of the Buddha within the relics,

[94] Sarkisyanz, *op. cit.*, p. 42.

[95] *Ibid.* Sarkisyanz quotes Paul Mus as saying that it was largely through the Bodhisattva ethos that "Buddhism developed from an ethical sect into one of the *politically* most effective ethical systems in the world."

[96] *Ibid.*, p. 44.

[97] E. g., *Dhammarājā, Dhammiko Dhammarājā, Mahādhammarājā, Mahā-sudassana, Mahāsattva, Bodhisattva, Cakkavatti (Cakravartin), Bodhisattvāvatara, Metteyya (Maitreya), Buddharājā*, et al.

[98] Gokhale, *op. cit.*, p. 22.

it is incomprehensible, accepted only by faith, made real only through enlightenment. It is the savaka-sangha, a spiritual community, invisible to all, whose members are known to none. It is a community of attainment where all striving has ceased. It is perceived in time but not limited by it; it occupies space but cannot be confined. It exists everywhere and in each place. It exists now and is eternal. No man is far from it, yet it remains unseen. To some, it seems fulfilled already, but this is blindness to suffering and to ignorance, especially their own. To others, it has no reality, for they place no hope in release from bondage, including their own. It is a city in which each learns from all and where none is lost. It is a community in which attainment has been reached, yet the horizons are unlimited. Here the glory of impermanence is understood, for each imagination has been opened to infinity. Here possession has no meaning, for no one is in need. Here fear is unknown, for love regards each person as himself.

The suttas, the commentaries, the chronicles, and a host of other testimonies bespeak of this City, yet no one who writes has more than glimpsed its possibility. The symbol of the Bodhi-tree, under which enlightenment first shone forth, is a primary image of the distance and of the closeness between wisdom and ignorance, between freedom and enslavement. In the epiphany symbolized by it we see the soil must be readied each time. The Buddha's visits to Lanka were to prepare yet another land for its transplant and growth. The vision told by the chronicler is of miracles taking place when preparation had occurred. "Hardly had he let it leave his hands but it rose up eighty cubits into the air, and floating thus it sent forth glorious rays of six colours."[99] "And while they all gazed, there grew, springing from it, eight shoots; and they stood there, young Bodhi-trees four cubits high."[100]

The glory of its springing forth and the tragedy that men remain ignorant is the essence of the chronicle's tale. The Wheel of the Law has been turned, yet men prefer to remain in Samsara. Dharma-vijaya has been shown as the way, but conquest continues through force. The unity which exists as a present reality is spurned, as men still war against each other. The kings whose freedom could bring liberation now are everywhere, yet each lives in fear of its consequences. The city where righteousness could be known is at hand, though no one would be its first citizen. Men settle for the accumulation of merit and the promise of heaven, even while the peace of Nibbana is more blissful still.

Yet it remains the genius of the Buddhist imagination that men must begin somewhere; therefore, no place of origin is despised. There will come a time when even relics will be extinguished (*dhātu-parinibbāna*), for the full presence will be known; in the meanwhile, these point the way. A time will unfold in which no monarchs are needed, for each will have achieved order by himself; though kings are needed yet. Finally, the ideal social order will have emerged, as each will have become righteous; though at present men still strain to perceive its configurations and to reject its demands.

[99] *Mahāvaṃsa*, p. 132.
[100] *Ibid.*, p. 133.

Religious Symbolism and Political Change in Ceylon[1]

By Gananath Obeyesekere

One of the fascinating problems in a sociological study of the "higher" religions is the manner in which the doctrinal or theological corpus has been "transformed"—to use Weber's term—on the behavioural level. Such doctrinal transformations, it can often be presumed, occur under the pressure of human needs or motives and/or through the operation of social structural and economic variables. Theravada Buddhism is doubly fascinating from this point of view because some of its major doctrinal postulates seem to go counter to the religious needs of the masses as we understand them from the cross-cultural evidence, e.g., the concept of *nirvana* with its notion of the extinction of personality and the cessation of all Being; that of *anatta*, or the doctrine that there is no permanent soul or "self" outside of the phenomenal 'I'; the devaluation of magic and a personal deity, and in its place an Enlightened Being or Buddha who, in so far as he is no longer alive, cannot assist the worshipper in any direct manner. Finally, though the existence of various types of deities are recognized, their power is necessarily curtailed by the doctrinal theory of *karma*, the predominant if not sole determinant of ('samsaric') events.

Recent social science studies of Theravada Buddhism indicate that the kind of transformations and reinterpretations of doctrinal Buddhism first spotlighted by Weber[2] have indeed occurred on the behavioural level; e.g., Ames,[3] de

[1] This paper was published in *Modern Ceylon Studies*, Vol. I, No. 1, University of Ceylon, 1970, pp. 43-63. It was originally prepared in 1966 for a Wenner-Gren Foundation Seminar and subsequently revised. I wish to acknowledge the criticism of my colleagues who attended the *Ceylon Studies Seminar* where this paper in substantially its present form was read on 8th June, 1969. I have to specially thank my friends Kitsiri Malalgoda and Tissa Fernando who helped me in various ways and K. H. Jayasinghe who referred me to the political pamphlet entitled "How Sirima's Government Fell." I regret that lack of knowledge of German prevented me from using Bechert's book *Buddhismus, Staat und Gesellschaft in den Landern des Theravada-Buddhismus.*

[2] Max Weber, *Religion of India*, Glencoe, Illinois, The Free Press, 1958.

[3] Michael Ames, "Ideological and Social Change in Ceylon," *Human Organization*, Vol. 22, Spring 1963, pp. 45-53.

Young,[4] Kaufman,[5] Leach,[6] Obeyesekere,[7] Spiro,[8] Wriggins,[9] Yalman.[10] Yet most of these studies deal with Buddhism as it is practiced in contemporary South Asian *peasant* societies, except Ames[11] and Wriggins.[12] My intention is to assume a peasant baseline for studying the changes that have occurred in Buddhism as a result of massive social changes, specially political changes in recent times. In order to do this we have to shift our focus from the village to the urban and the city context.

For the purposes of this paper the most important of these political changes was the transfer of political power to the Ceylonese with the granting of independence in 1948. The initial political dominance of the Christian population and the city "middle class" soon disappeared, and there was by 1956 an effective transference of political power to the Sinhalese speaking Buddhist population.

The details are available in Wriggins *Ceylon: Dilemmas of a New Nation*,[13] and in Singer *The Emerging Elite*.[14] There is practically no chance of reversal of this trend; the dominant ethos is and will continue to be Sinhalese Buddhist. If the present political and religious trends continue Buddhism may be officially declared the state religion within a decade. For all practical purposes it is the state religion today.

The problem of my paper is as follows: with massive political changes concomitant changes in Buddhism, on the behavioural level, would have occurred. I propose to examine some of these changes, and the political and social "conditions" that have produced them.

Let me illustrate with one example the kind of religious change on the symbolic level which I am concerned with in the present analysis. I drive along a major highway in Colombo, formerly known as Turret Road, but recently renamed Dharmapala Mawata, after Anagarika Dharmapala, a prominent Buddhist leader in modern times. A short distance and I turn right and then come to a

---

[4] John E. de Young, *Village Life in Modern Thailand*, Berkeley, University of California Press, 1955.

[5] H. K. Kaufman, *Bankhaud, A Community Study in Thailand*, New York, J. J. Angustin, 1960.

[6] E. R. Leach, "Pulleyar and the Lord Buddha," *Psychoanalysis and the Psychoanalytic Review*, Vol. 49, 1962, pp. 80-102.

[7] Gananath Obeyesekere, "The Great Tradition and the Little in the Perspective of Sinhalese Buddhism," *Journal of Asian Studies*, Vol. XXII, No. 2, 1963, pp. 139-153.

[8] Melford E. Spiro, "Religious Systems as Culturally Constituted Defense Mechanisms," *Context and Meaning in Cultural Anthropology*, pp. 100-112, Glencoe, The Free Press, 1965.

[9] Howard W. Wriggins, *Ceylon: Dilemmas of a New Nation*, Princeton, 1960.

[10] Nur Yalman, "The Structure of Sinhalese Healing Rituals," *Aspects of Religion in South Asia*, Special issue, *Journal of Asian Studies*, Vol. XXIII, pp. 115-150, 1964.

[11] Michael M. Ames, "Religion, Politics and Economic Development in Ceylon: An Interpretation of the Weber Thesis," *Symposium on New Approaches to the Study of Religion*, Melford E. Spiro, Editor, pp. 61-76, Seattle, 1963.

[12] Wriggins, *Ceylon: Dilemmas of a New Nation*.

[13] *Ibid.*

[14] Marshall Singer, *The Emerging Elite*, Cambridge, Mass., M. I. T. Press, 1964.

roundabout at a point where three major roads meet. Behind the roundabout is a large *bo* tree. On this roundabout are erected four huge concrete maps of Ceylon about five feet in height; they face the four directions in a square. In the middle of each map is engraved an ethical precept of Doctrinal Buddhism (1) *mudita*, "sympathetic joy," (2) *upekka*, "equanimity," (3) *karuna*, "compassion," (4) *metta*, "universal love." On the top of each map is painted the national emblem of the Sinhalese, a highly stylized lion, with a sword held aloft in one paw. This structure was erected by a prominent member of the Ceylon Buddhist Congress, a powerful Buddhist organization whose leadership largely consists of middle-class, professional and business persons. Its power is largely due to its wealth, its elite membership, its highly vocal leadership with political influence in national politics. It has practically no influence on the level of peasants many of whom have no idea of its very existence.

On the cognitive level it is unlikely that a Sinhalese Buddhist would see anything discordant in this roundabout. Yet for a sociologist there is something unusual. Firstly, there are four universalistic Buddhist concepts of sympathetic joy, equanimity, compassion, universal love; these "universal" concepts which from the doctrinal point of view are ethical norms for all mankind are "contained" within a map of Ceylon, i.e., the universalistic concepts are embodied in a particularistic (national) framework. Moreover, the painting of the lion, a predatory, carnivorous creature grasping a sword, a symbol of violence, seems to contradict the lofty doctrinal sentiments. The emblem of the lion in turn relates to the origin myth of the Sinhalese race. This myth relates that the King of Kalinga had a daughter, who according to prophesy would elope with the King of the beasts. In order to ward off the prophecy the King kept his daughter confined, but one day she managed to escape and joined a caravan of merchants. While the caravan was passing the forest, it was attacked by a lion who carried away the princess and cohabited with her. Thus we have the theme of bestiality. According to the cultural norms of any group a bestial union cannot produce "good" offspring. The result of this union is Sinhabahu ('the lion arm') a male and Sinhasivali, a female. This pair grew up and became aware of their "unusual" life circumstances. One day when the father was away on a hunt, the son removed his mother and sister and fled to his grandfather's kingdom, where he was welcomed as the heir apparent. The son married his sister. The theme of bestiality is compounded by that of incest. Meanwhile the angry lion, seeing the loss of his family wrought destruction on adjacent villages. The son kills the father—bestiality, incest, parricide. Nothing good could be expected of the union of brother and sister with a history of bestiality and parricide. They had an offspring, Vijaya who with his murderous group of 500 friends, acted very much like his grandfather, the lion—killing and hurting innocent people. The King, Sinhabahu, banished his son and his followers. With their heads shaved they were put on a ship—the watery rebirth that symbolically eliminates the "sins" of the past. They landed in Ceylon and founded a new race—the Sinhalese, or "the lion race."

Now we can come back to the "roundabout" near Dharmapala Mawata, Colombo. Juxtaposed with the highly abstract universal ethical concepts from doctrinal Buddhism are their concrete particularistic opposites—bestiality, incest, parricide, violence. Both sets are contained within the map of Ceylon. What is being expressed here on the symbolical level in this somewhat ungainly concrete edifice?

On the one hand it represents a shift of power that has occurred on the political level—political power is effectively in the hands of the Sinhalese Buddhist population. Hence the juxtaposition of the predatory lion symbolism (Sinhalese) with the abstract ethical concepts of a universal religion (Buddhism). Ceylon is "claimed" for the Sinhalese Buddhists, by the Sinhalese Buddhists. This of course may be denied by the other religious and racial groups, but we are not interested in that at the moment.

Secondly, let me reiterate that the Buddhist concepts are highly abstract ones from the *doctrinal* corpus, not from the cultural repertoire of the mass of peasants. They are written in their *pali* form (*pali* is a language in which the Theravada doctrines are written). This in my opinion expresses a cultural shift that has occurred concomitant with the political shift. Let me briefly explain this cultural shift.

In early British times effective control of education was in the hands of Christian mission schools. These mission schools, both Catholic and Protestant, were modelled on the lines of the English public school system and included such phenomena as "houses," prefects, cricket, "big matches," etc., as well as the public school syllabuses and curricula. Later (post 1880) Buddhist mission schools sponsored by the Buddhist Theosophical Society founded by an American, Col. Olcott, and the Mahabodhi Society founded by Anagarika Dharmapala also founded new schools. But the model they adopted was the missionary public school model—all the way from cricket to the curriculum. Even the names were based on the Christian—instead of St. Peters, St. Thomas' or Bishop's College, you had Ananda, Nalanda, Rahula or Mahabodhi. A Buddhist catechism and a Buddhist flag were devised by Olcott. The Buddhist catechism has gone out of vogue; but the flag remains as a highly cathected symbol of Buddhist national identity. Few are aware of the recent American origin of this sacred symbol. The teachers who were recruited to Buddhist schools were often originally educated in mission schools. Hence there was a dissemination of Victorian-Protestant ethical ideas into the culture of the elite Buddhists. In so far as political and economic dominance was Christian, there was motivation for the *cathexis* of these norms by Buddhists. Hence today Buddhist sexual morality, its monogamous marriage ideals, and divorce rules are highly cathected derivatives from Protestantism. Historically it should be noted that these ideals were never exclusively dominant in any period of Buddhism in any of the Theravada societies of South Asia prior to the 20th century. Alongside the cathexis of norms there was an adoption of organizational "forms" from Christianity—Young Men's (Women's) Buddhist Associations, Buddhist Army Chaplains, Sunday Schools for Buddhists (till 1965), missionary organizations and various types of Buddhist associations. Since traditional Buddhism lacked any formal modern organizational apparatus, the existent Protestant models were adopted by Buddhists. Thus contemporary Buddhism could conveniently be called *Protestant* Buddhism.

The term "Protestant Buddhism" in my usage has two meanings. (a) As we have pointed out many of its norms and organizational forms are historical derivatives from Protestant Christianity. (b) More importantly, from the contemporary point of view, it is a protest *against* Christianity and its associated Western political dominance prior to independence. Thus, for example, those very norms that were derived from Western Victorian Protestantism were thrown back at the 20th century West—Westerners are believed to be sexually lax, and there is a general condemnation of "Western" values. Very few elite Buddhists are aware of the fact that in isolated traditional Buddhist villages, sexual morality and divorce may be far more "lax" than in many communities in Europe or the U.S.A. Whenever these facts are made known they are condemned as un-Buddhistic, immoral and even untraditional!

The intellectual protest against Christianity was facilitated by Western scholarship, specially the translation and interpretation of texts by the scholars associated with the Pali Text Society. The propagandists of the intellectual Buddhist movement were trained in mission schools. Doctrinal Buddhism was held up as a kind of Theosophy, as it is today with intellectuals; a rational religion without a Saviour or a cult, devoid of "superstitions." This intellectual revivalist movement however had to contend with an obvious contradiction in peasant culture with its array of demonological cults, beliefs in sorcery and magic. Thus the resurrection of doctrinal Buddhism, involved a demythologising of peasant beliefs and a *rationalization* of peasant cults. I emphasize *rationalization* for it is not that these beliefs are done away with. They are elided of their "vulgar" qualities, they are made more "respectable." Against the abstractions of doctrinal Buddhism are counterposed the concrete "needs" of the believer and their satisfaction in ritual and worship even among urban Buddhists. The predatory lion juxtaposed against the universalistic norms of *pali suttas* are only one aspect of a larger process.

Let us briefly get back to our concrete slabs to illustrate the third set of processes of change being reflected therein. The edifice has been erected at the traffic roundabout. Though strictly speaking this edifice is not an object of worship, nevertheless it is located in the "hub" of events; not in the isolation of a monastery, a cave or hill temple. Since this edifice is not one of worship it is time we left it and drove a mile towards another, even more crowded roundabout where Darley Road meets McCallum Road. Here we come across a Buddha image erected as the roundabout. This statue was erected in the 1950's; the manner in which it was erected is interesting. Near the roundabout is St. Joseph's College, a well known Catholic public school. Its one-time rector was Father Le Goc, an influential Catholic priest. When he died the Colombo Municipal Council gave permission to the Catholics to erect a pillar in his memory at this same roundabout. The pillar was in fact erected, but one morning "pious" Buddhists in the area had also planted there a Buddha statue. This action, ignoring the obviously hostile motives that went into it, was illegal and created a furor. But Father Le Goc was "displaced" and the Buddha came to stay there permanently. The symbolic significance of the act is obvious: it expresses the displacement of Catholicism as a manifest public force and the substitution of Buddhism in its place. But there is a deeper implication here which we must now pursue.

We leave Colombo city and travel in the Southern direction through the densely populated West coast areas of Ceylon along Galle Road—Ceylon's major highway. Before we leave Colombo we notice that a Buddha statue and a temple have been erected at the corner of the former Turf Club—illegally by a squatter monk. As we reach Lunava, 10 miles from Colombo we see a Buddha at another roundabout; in the next town, Panadura, a huge gilt Buddha is erected at a fork in Galle Road; in Kalutara, another town, there is another cement-Buddha. The concrete edifice we spoke of earlier is no fortuitous thing; elsewhere at other roundabouts in the urban west coast, Buddha statues have sprung up. We then remember, that there is a Buddha statue erected in the premises of Radio Ceylon; another has been erected in front of the new and impressive seven story Irrigation Department Headquarters, constructed only in 1963. Buddha statues have sprung up everywhere in urban Ceylon. Superficially there may be nothing strange in this, but for the fact that the Buddha, was never represented *spatially* in this way, traditionally. The Buddha, to put it metaphorically, has been brought to the market place.

THE SYMBOLIC SIGNIFICANCE OF SPATIAL SHIFTS

The significance of "social space" has been recently discussed by Warner.[15] In his discussion of the organization of the American cemetery, Warner shows that the size of the grave stones reflect the relative statuses of the respective members of the elementary family. He also shows how persons who have recently moved up the class ladder sometimes remove the gravestones of their parents from lower class burial grounds to upper class ones. Similarly the movement of Buddha statues from the traditional isolated repositories to the "market place" suggests important antecedent socio-political changes in urban Ceylon, some of which we have discussed earlier.

Traditionally the ideal way of building a temple or any religious edifice is to ensure a spatial separation of the religious edifice from the human community. Analogously the incumbents of these temples—the Buddhist monks—were spatially separated from the peasant laity. For religious worship the peasants went to the temple; for certain parish tasks like participation in almsgiving rites, recital of texts (*parittas*) and funeral rites the monks went to the village. The spatial separation of the edifice and the incumbent from the human community reflects a behavioural manifestation of a central Buddhist doctrinal value. Briefly stated, the Buddha and rites associated with him deal with the other-worldly

[15] Lloyd W. Warner, *The Living and the Dead*, New Haven, Yale University Press, 1959, see also Lloyd W. Warner, *The Family of God*, New Haven, 1961.

interests of the masses. Furthermore, salvation (*nirvana*) involves as its prerequisite an emancipation from the social structure, i.e., emancipation from the attachment to the world. These ideal doctrinal postulates are manifest in the spatial separation of monk and temple from the peasant and the village. It is also manifest in the *vestment* of the monk (vestment, as I define it, is the special garb of any religious specialist, which symbolizes his status). The monk's patched yellow robe, his begging bowl and his shaven head symbolize the *formal ideal* of renunciation of the world. If the Buddha and the associated symbolism have to do with other-worldly interests, not so with the *devas*, the powerful deities of the Sinhalese Buddhist pantheon. These beings are intercessionary deities who assist the worshipper with material weal—good crops, health, etc. in one's present existence. Then there are demons (*yakkas*) and spirits who are entirely malevolent and cause illness and misfortune on humans. The placation of *devas* and *yakkas* are by different religious specialists (*kapurala, kattadirala, adura*).[16] The spatial separation discussed earlier in reference to the village and the temple never occurs in the latter. The *devas* and *yakkas* are often placated in the precincts of the village; they may even inhabit, or protect the village. The religious specialists of these cults live in the village. They wear the normal garb of the peasant and have lay roles; only when they perform rituals for these respective deities do they wear a special vestment. After the ritual is over they *divest* themselves and fall back into lay statuses and roles. Thus the *devas* and *yakkas* are directly associated with the material interests of the masses.

In the urban context described above a spatial shift has occurred—the Buddha is being brought into the hub of events. What briefly are the underlying factors responsible for this spatial shift? (1) Firstly, the political changes discussed earlier—it represents for all to see the idea of a Buddhist nation; it is the national religion. The Buddha images and other edifices located everywhere are visible public symbols of Buddhist nationalism like a flag or the totem animal in Durkheim's analysis of Australian aboriginal religion.[17] (2) Secondly, in politics and in political controversy, Buddhist monks have had to come into the open as a political force. Their active this-worldly involvement in the political world has occurred. The Buddha in the market place expresses, on a symbolic level, the involvement of Buddhist activists in the world. (3) There is thirdly, I think, a psychological fact analogous to that described as deprivation by Barber[18] and Aberle[19] for nativistic movements. The social psychological factor involved could

[16] Gananath Obeyesekere, "The Great Tradition and the Little in the Perspective of Sinhalese Buddhism," see also, Gananath Obeyesekere, "The Buddhist Pantheon in Ceylon and its Extensions."

[17] Emile Durkheim, *The Elementary Forms of the Religious Life*, Glencoe, The Free Press, 1915.

[18] Bernard Barber, "Acculturation and Messianic Movements," *American Sociological Review*, Vol. VII, 1941, pp. 663-669.

[19] D. F. Aberle, "A Note on Relative Deprivation Theory as applied to Millenial and Other Movements," Sylvia L. Thrupp (Ed.) *Millenial Dreams in Action, Supplement* II-*Comparative Studies in Society and History*, Mounton 1962, pp. 209-214.

be (somewhat simply) described as a lowering of self worth of the Buddhists as a result of deprivations consequent on three waves of foreign invasion. Rapidly, however, political power falls into the hands of the Buddhists. An attempt is made by Buddhists to regain their self *esteem or self worth*; in the process a kind of *reaction-formation* or *overcompensation* has occurred. This is manifested in another aspect of spatial symbolism—the size of the statues. The edifices in the market place are generally huge, though aesthetically crude, constructions. Though there is traditional precedence for this in Buddhist sculpture, the large number of these huge edifices constructed in one generation suggest an attempt at overcompensation. For example, a statue, which is said to be the largest in the world has recently been erected in Matara, South Ceylon. In Colombo the tallest building was a Protestant Church; recently a national Buddhist organization erected an edifice to supercede this. In Kurunegala the Protestant Bishop had an impressive church built; another Buddhist organization has now decided to erect a huge Buddha statue on top of a hill adjacent this church so as to completely dwarf the latter. Thus the size of edifices is an attempt to regain the self esteem of the Buddhists through overcompensation, manifest in spatial symbolism. Incidentally the "model" for emulation is once again Christian. Christian missionaries planted churches in centres of Buddhist worship all over Ceylon.[20]

It would be argued that the statues planted in public places, are indicative of the "public character" of contemporary Buddhism as the national religion and does not signify any real attitudinal change on the part of urban Buddhists. That the spatial shift that we have described is indicative of a change in attitude is suggested very strongly if we shift our focus from the "market place" to the home. Here too a symbolic shift has taken place. Buddha images are enshrined in a special part of middle class houses, called by English speaking Sinhalese as a "shrine-room" or in Sinhalese, as "*Budu ge*," (lit. "Buddha house".) The shrine room is an important innovation and a departure from tradition. Traditionally Sinhalese peasant households lit coconut oil lamps in domestic shrines for the *devas* every evening, or on Wednesdays and Saturdays, the special (*kemmura*) days, for *pujas* for deities. The idea was to seek the protection of the *deva* for the inmates of the household. Thus the *devas* were also domestic deities, presiding over and protecting the inhabitants of a household. The Buddha was never a domestic deity in this sense; he was never propitiated or represented in the household shrines. His images were in temples spatially isolated not only from the village but also from the household. Instead of the Buddha, pictures of the *arhat* Sivali were kept in the household; it was Sivali and not the Buddha who was viewed as capable of bringing material prosperity and blessings for the household. But Sivali has been displaced and the Buddha has taken his place in the domestic shrine.[21] If the movement of the Buddha statues to the market place

[20] This is not unique to Buddhism and Christianity but probably true of any proselytising religion in a position of dominance.

[21] There were many pragmatic reasons why the shrine room could not have occurred traditionally. The shrine room has pictures and images of the Buddha. Traditionally this

indicates the involvement of Buddhism with the world and the acquisition of political power in the hands of the Buddhists, the shrine in the home indicates that an attitudinal change has occurred among urban Buddhists. Urban Buddhists subjectively perceive that the "Buddha" is somehow involved in the affairs of the world. This practice is near universal with middle-class Buddhists. That the change is a dramatic one is apparent when we compare urban Buddhism in respect of this change with peasant Buddhism. In two traditional peasant villages in which I have done extensive field work—Madagama in the Southern Province and Laggala in the Central Province—there were no domestic shrines for the Buddha. In one village—Ihala Biyanwila—only fifteen miles from Colombo there were domestic shrines for the gods Skanda and Huniyan but rarely for the Buddha. This change I believe does not imply a change in respect of how the Buddha is perceived. In both urban and rural Ceylon people know, on the conscious level at least, that the Buddha cannot grant favours, or intercede on behalf of the worshipper. The prayers uttered before domestic shrines are no different from those uttered in temples. What then does the domestic Buddha shrine signify? It signifies, in my opinion, the emergent political and social self consciousness of urban Buddhists. The model, it should be noted, is once again Christian—in this case Catholic. It is also very likely that the idea of the *Budu ge* was popularized if not introduced by the Anagarika Dharmapala, whose role we shall discuss later.

THE ROLE OF THE MONK

That the symbolic shifts that we have described are more political and social rather than economic are apparent when we examine the role of the monk. The involvement of Buddhism with the world does not imply so much a developing economic ethic—though this may eventually occur—but a developing political and social ethic. With increasing involvement with the world one would expect a greater "parish orientation" in the role of the urban monk. This is indeed the case, for monks are increasingly involved in political roles ("right" and "left"), and also in social services, and missionary activity. However a great deal of ambiguity exists in respect of economic activity, for economic development and technological advances are perceived as aspects of Western scientific materialism and therefore devalued. Thus while there is a strong positive political involvement of Buddhism, the attitude to economic development is either ambiguous or negative.

The involvement of the monk in the world is an intensification of the traditional parish roles he had to perform. From the point of view of the public this produces an ambivalent and paradoxical attitude towards the monk. This has to do with the contradiction between the ideal norms of world renunciation as a

would be rare, since cheap mass produced pictures and plastic images of the Buddha are a modern phenomenon. In my opinion even pictures of the *arhat* Sivali are an early 20th century innovation.

measure of piety, and the contradiction of that ideal in the actual urban monk role. The ideal of renunciation is a continuing value in Buddhist society; traditionally as well as today the ideal monk is one who has retreated into a forest hermitage, engaged in solitary meditation. The monk who lives in the village temple, performing his normal parish roles, is viewed as being ritually inferior to the ascetic monk. With the greater political involvement of the urban monk, there is a greater public criticism of his virtue. Thus during the last general election campaign the right wing group continually condemned the left wing monks as *dussila* (unvirtuous), while the left wing used the identical epithet to characterize right wing monks. It is likely that as far as the general public is concerned both left and right wing monks are considered *dussila*. In conversation with middle class Sinhalese Buddhists one is struck by the open contempt and abuse directed against politically active monks, and the highly salacious gossip that circulate about their "immorality."

To sum up, the political involvement of the urban monk has intensified greatly the public ambivalence that even traditionally existed towards the "temple" monk. But this involves a paradox, for the monk is perceived as the visible symbol of the Buddhist political nationalism and therefore respected. Many Buddhists attempt to resolve the ambiguity by saying "we respect the yellow robe (the "vestment") but not the person"; but it is doubtful whether this rationalization resolves the underlying psychological ambivalence. My own view is that recent trends in public attitudes to the monk are one of increasing disrespect for his this-worldly orientation, rather than respect towards him as a symbol of political nationalism. In fact there is a group known as the *vinaya vardhana samitiya* (society for rejuvenating the discipline) with fair support in the more urbanized villages, which has as its avowed objective the purification of the *Sangha* (order of monks) by attempting to enforce the *vinaya* (traditional rules of discipline).[22]

The statement "we respect the yellow robe but not the person," implies the public perception of the importance of the *vestment* of the monk. The monk's vestment—the robe that is "patched" and the begging bowl are symbols of the ideal of world renunciation. Twenty-five years ago it was a common sight in the morning for monks to go out begging for alms as it is today in Thailand and Burma. "Begging for alms" was a public symbolic validation of the ideal of renunciation of the world; it did not imply that the monastery was not self sufficient in terms of food. It was a "cultural performance" of an ideal role. Today hardly anywhere in Ceylon can one see monks on the "alms round"; the begging bowl and the alms round as public visible symbols of renunciation are absent. Though there are many factors at work here, one important factor is probably the increasing involvement of the monk in the world, specifically a political involvement. Thus with the changes in role there is a concomitant change in the vestment.

[22] Ames, "Ideological and Social Change in Ceylon."

THE "ANAGARIKA" SYMBOL AND THE "ANAGARIKA" ROLE

The ambivalence towards the monk, we said, was based on the contradiction between the ideal of renunciation on the one hand and the increased this-worldly parish and political roles of the urban monk on the other. This contradiction is largely eliminated in the lay Buddhist role, because the layman, according to both doctrinal and behavioural norms, is not expected to renounce the world. How is it possible, without any contradiction or ambivalence, to effect a this-worldly asceticism, congruent with the changing political and economic landscape of Ceylon? The bridge is effected in the symbol of a great political and religious leader of modern Ceylon—the Anagarika Dharmapala. If ideally the symbol of the monk represents world renunciation and the layman world involvement, the *anagarika* represents an attempt to renounce the world while living in the world. The *anagarika* (meaning "the homeless") has a special vestment, a white robe, but worn differently from that of the monk. However his head is not shaved unlike that of the monk—symbolizing his greater involvement with the world.

The *anagarika* like the monk is *brahmacari*, i.e., committed to sexual absti-nence; he also practices the ascetic renunciation (the ten *silas*) incumbent on novices. Yet he is neither novice, nor monk; his unique status permits him to engage in certain types of this-worldly activity difficult in theory for the monk to perform: political, social service and missionary activity. The *anagarika* role also resolves the moral ambivalence associated with the temple monk. He has given up the lay life nevertheless and the mundane satisfaction associated with it—his is a this-worldly asceticism reminiscent of Calvinism. However the social context in which the *anagarika* role is performed is different from the Calvinist, so that the asceticism of the *anagarika* is directed towards social and political goals. The *anagarika* status is also an innovation in Sinhalese Buddhism and its significance can best be appreciated in the context of the socio-political changes outlined earlier.

The first person to adopt the *anagarika* role was Anagarika Dharmapala, who within thirty years of his death, has become transformed into a symbol of mod-ern Sinhalese Buddhist nationalism. Anagarika Dharmapala was born in 1864 as Don David Hevavitharana, the son of a wealthy furniture dealer belonging to the *goigama* (farmer) caste. He was educated in leading mission schools in Colombo. In 1881, coming under the influence of the theosophists, Col. Olcott and Madame Blavatsky and prominent Buddhist monks who were engaged in a famous religious debate with Christians, he adopted the role of *anagarika*. He changed his "Western" name and adopted the name of Dharmapala ("guardian of the doctrine"). Ten years later he founded the *Mahabodhi Society*, the goal of which was resuscitation of Buddhism in India and in Ceylon. In 1906 he founded the *Sinhala Baudhaya*—"the Sinhalese Buddhist"—an influential Sinhalese news paper. In Ceylon his avowed goal was to rehabilitate Buddhism and the Sinhalese race which had become denationalized, de-religious, and degenerated owing to Western conquest and Western influence. A hard hitting, vitriolic polemecist he was fluent in both English and Sinhalese. He ridiculed mercilessly Sinhalese "upper classes" who had become "Westernized" and idealized the glories of the Sinhalese past. His goals, idealism, polemicism, and nationalism are part of the current ideology of modern Buddhism. Today a special day of the year is allocated to him—Dharmapala Day—when processions carrying his image are paraded in practically every large city. Streets all over urban Ceylon have been named after him. Though in the last years of his life he became a fully ordained monk and adopted a new name—Sri Devamitta Dharmapala—he is known and remembered as Anagarika Dharmapala. His symbolic significance is not as monk but as *anagarika*.

The Anagarika Dharmapala was a tireless advocate of political and social reform. "I have to be active and activity means agitation according to constitutional methods."[23] He held up the past glories of the Sinhalese as an ideal worth resurrecting. "No nation in the world has had a brilliant history than ourselves."[24] There exists no race on the earth today that has had a more glorious, triumphant record of victory than the Sinhalese."[25] The present degradation is due to evil Western influence—both missionary and colonialism. The country, as he perceives it, is a Sinhalese Buddhist one—there is hardly a place for Tamils and Muslims who are viewed as exploiters. The Christians are condemned as meat eaters of "low caste." "The country of the Sinhalese should be governed by the Sinhalese."[26] While he held up the ideal of Christ himself, the general bias in his polemics is for a Sinhalese Buddhist nation.

In reading the published writings of Anagarika Dharmapala one is struck by the complete contrast between his style and the impersonal tone of the Buddhist *Suttas*, and the almost clinical detachment of the *Abhidhamma*. Dharmapala's style is much like that of Protestant missionaries in its tone of personal involvement and invective.

I quote several examples:

    (a) In 1902 he writes: "The sweet gentle Aryan children of an ancient historic race are sacrificed at the altar of whisky-drinking, beef-eating belly-god of heathenism. How long, Oh! How long will unrighteousness last in Ceylon."[27]

    (b) "Practices which were an abomination to the ancient noble Sinhalese have today become tolerated."[28]

    (c) "Arise, awake, unite and join the army of Holiness and Peace and defeat the hosts of evil."[29]

---

[23] Anagarika Dharmapala, *Return to Righteousness: A Collection of Speeches, Essays and Letters of Anagarika Dharmapala*. A. Guruge: editor, Government Press, Colombo, 1965, p. 735.

[24] *Ibid.*, p. 566.

[25] *Ibid.*, p. 481.

[26] *Ibid.*, p. LVII.

[27] *Ibid.*, p. 484.

[28] *Ibid.*, p. 494.

[29] *Ibid.*, p. 660.

Thus the *anagarika*, trained in mission schools has imbibed along with his hatred of the missions, a dialectic used by the missionaries to castigate Buddhism. He set the style for a dialectic that has become a norm among Buddhists nationalists today.

The *anagarika's* scattered writings have just been collated and reprinted in part. His significance for contemporary Buddhists is however not as a person but as a symbol of (a) a Sinhalese Buddhist rejuvenated Ceylon (b) an asceticism directed towards this-worldly activity. His transformation is much like the transformation of Lincoln, the individual, into the symbolic Lincoln.[30] The *anagarika* symbol is a product of the times; had he been born in a different era he would have vanished without making any impact. In 20th century Ceylon, Buddhism provided the focus of national unity. In the process it was inevitable that it had to get involved in the world. The model for this involvement was a Protestant model: the *anagarika* symbol is the modern Sinhalese Buddhist analogue of an early Calvinist type of reformism with its increasing this-worldly asceticism. Though Anagarika Dharmapala is more a symbol than a person for most contemporary Buddhists, the *anagarika* role is a function of a specific socio-political context. In the Buddhist Pali texts, the term *anagarika* (homeless) was exclusively applied for *monks. Anagarika* and monk were equivalent; the resurrection of the term *anagarika* by Dharmapala in 1881 to designate a specific status intermediate between monk and layman was an innovation. Its popular acceptance was due to "need": in this case the necessity for a "homeless life" (*anagarika*) while living in the world.

The life and work of Anagarika Dharmapala anticipated much of contemporary Buddhism. In his Sinhalese writings his audience was never the peasant; it was an educated Sinhalese speaking or bilingual intelligensia. He enhanced their sense of self worth and, in the political changes of the mid-century, provided a "charter" for modern Buddhism. Let us consider some aspects of the charter he provided for contemporary Buddhists.

(a) A this-worldly asceticism

He castigated the laziness of the Sinhalese, emphasized thrift, saving, hardwork. He exhorted people to reject the propitiation of *devas*; to worship the Buddha daily at home and every week in the temple. He exhorted parents to get their children interested in meditational (*sil*) activity (generally accepted in contemporary Buddhism, but an innovation at that time for, traditionally, such activity was confined to old persons). He condemned again and again the consumption of meat and alcohol (though singularly silent about fish).

(b) A code of lay ethics

Buddhist doctrine has no systematic code of lay ethics, though the rules of conduct for the order (*sangha*) are minutely regulated, great emphasis being placed on personal decorum, good manners. As far as the layman was concerned

---

[30] Warner, *The Living and the Dead*, p. 248.

only broad generalizations were available in texts like the *Sigalovada Sutta.* This absence of specificity regarding lay ethics facilitated the spread of Buddhism among peasant societies with diverse and even contradictory moral codes. However in 1898 the Anagarika Dharmapala laid down a systematic code for the laity in a pamphlet published in Sinhalese entitled "The Daily Code for the Laity." The nineteenth edition appeared in 1958: 49,500 copies of this work were sold. Rules on the following subjects were minutely regulated.[31]

1 The manner of eating food (25 rules)

2 Chewing betel (6)

3 Wearing clean clothes (5)

4 How to use the lavatory (4)

5 How to behave while walking on the road (10)

6 How to behave in public gatherings (19)

7 How females should conduct themselves (30)

8 How children should conduct themselves (18)

9 How the laity should conduct themselves before the *Sangha* (5)

10 How to behave in buses and trains (8)

11 What village protection societies should do (8)

12 On going to see sick persons (2)

13 Funerals (3)

14 The carters' code (6)

15 Sinhalese clothes (6)

16 Sinhalese names (2)

17 What teachers should do (11)

18 How servants should behave (9)

19 How festivities should be conducted (5)

20 How lay devotees (male and female) should conduct themselves in the temple (3)

21 How children should treat their parents (14)

22 Domestic ceremonies (1)

A total of 200 rules guiding lay conduct under twenty-two heads have been devised by the Anagarika. In examining these rules several conclusions could be drawn.

(1) The pamphlet is addressed to a literate Sinhalese intelligensia: the

---

[31] Anagarika Dharmapala, *Dharmapala Lipi*, Govt. Press, Colombo, 1963, pp. 31-46.

kinds of proscriptive rules are those that peasants are generally given to, e.g., 'bad' eating, dress, and lavatory habits, indiscriminate betel chewing, use of impolite forms of address (though the Anagarika uses those same terms in a letter to one of his servants). This is a code of conduct for an "emerging Sinhalese elite."

(2) Alongside traditional norms of conduct are many Western norms. Even the condemnation of peasant manners is based on a Western yardstick. That is, the Anagarika attempted to formulate a code based on traditional as well as on the norms prevalent in the wealthy society in which he was reared. Here is an aspect of the larger process we have mentioned earlier; Protestant and Western norms have been cathected and assimilated as pure or ideal Sinhalese norms. In the case of the Anagarika it was specially interesting for his avowed intention was to reject Western ways. Yet regulations about the correct manner of using the fork and spoon are also given! Elsewhere, his admiration for the West breaks through the polemic and comes out into the open. "Europe is progressive. Her religion is kept in the background for one day in the week and for six days her people are following the dictates of modern science. Sanitation, aesthetic arts, electricity, etc., are what made Europeans and American people great. Asia is full of opium eaters, ganja smokers, degenerating sensualists, superstitions and religious fanatics. Gods and priests keep the people in ignorance."[32]

(c) Missionary Activity

The Anagarika Dharmapala, as pointed out earlier, was not only interested in rejuvenating Sinhalese Buddhism, but also in conquering the world for the Buddha *Dhamma*. However, he realized eventually that the Western barbarians were beyond hope, and confined missionary activity to India with fair success. The goals of the Anagarika were consistently realistic; in this respect they must be contrasted with the proselytization goals of the contemporary Buddhist missions. Contemporary missions are convinced that the West is waiting to be converted; the more realistic goals of converting Indians are neglected. One would have thought that conversion of the Hindu and Catholic population in Ceylon would be considered an urgent necessity by Buddhist missionaries, from their point of view. But little attention is given to this; Europe and America have to be converted. This is again an aspect of the "overcompensation" phenomenon noted earlier.

The Anagarika Dharmapala provided a 'role model' for a this-worldly asceticism for Buddhism. In his own day his influence on constitutional reform was negligible. His influence was with the "not yet emerged" Sinhalese elite (the village monk, the school teacher, the notary and the Ayurvedic physician) who, according to Wriggins, spearheaded the 1956 election which brought about a radical shift of power in Ceylon's politics. For them he provided a model for emulation—a national consciousness, a nativistic sense of past glory and present

---

[32] Anagarika Dharmapala, *Return to Righteousness*, p. 717.

degeneration, and very importantly, an ascetic involvement in this-worldly activity, not of an economic, but of a socio-political nature. Few people since his day have actually adopted the *anagarika* status with its associated vestment. But the *anagarika* role has come to stay. A this-worldly asceticism comprising of the puritan type code of morality is part of the higher code of urban elite Buddhism —a greater commitment to the doctrine, an emphasis on a "rigid" moral code, meditational activity for young and old, an intolerance towards other faiths, an identification of Ceylon with Buddhism and the Sinhalese language, and an involvement in social and political (though not economic) activity. However there is one important difference between the *anagarika* role symbolized by Anagarika Dharmapala and the contemporary adoption of that role. The *anagarika* status is a "bachelor" status; the contemporary "puritanism" by contrast is for all, including married persons. The Anagarika Dharmapala emphasized the doctrinal aspects of Buddhism; in accordance with the doctrine, he scorned the intercessionary powers of *devas* and demons. For elite Buddhists of today involved in the family and the larger society this is not easy, for the Buddha is not a conventional deity granting favours. Thus among the latter there is a greater dependence on *devas*, contradicting the doctrinal position which devaluates the power of these beings. Here we are dealing with an important psychological variable—a need for the *devas*. This is the subject of the next section of this paper.

POLITICAL CHANGE AND THE RELIGIOUS PANTHEON

The formal organization of the traditional Sinhalese Buddhist pantheon was based on feudal ideas. Since I have described the structure of the pantheon elsewhere,[33] it will suffice here if I briefly sketch its general outlines. The Buddha is the presidential deity of the pantheon; he is perceived as pure benevolence, yet he has no intercessory role in the affairs of the world. Below him are the guardian gods of Ceylon—Vishnu, Skanda, Nata, Vibisana, Saman and Goddess Pattini. They are protectors of the faith, and conventional deities who grant material favours to the devotee. Below them are lesser provincial deities; then there are malevolent demons, and lower down in the hierarchy mean spirits, ghosts and goblins. The pantheon is structured very much on the lines of the traditional feudal order. The lesser deities have *varan* (warrant) to do good or harm from the superior deities, as the officials of the feudal system had *varan* from their superiors. All *varan* ultimately devolves on the Buddha in the religious realm; as it devolved on the King in the political realm. Each deity has his *sima* (area of jurisdiction and authority) like feudal governors and officials. The lesser deities are viewed as a retinue of the greater deities. The kind of ritual (*tevava*) performed for the gods is practically identical with the traditional court ritual, also called *tevava*.

In the city, among the urban "middle class," conspicuous changes in the pantheon have occurred. These changes are broadly of two types:

[33] Obeyesekere, "The Great Tradition and the Little in the Perspective of Sinhalese Buddhism"; see also, "The Buddhist Pantheon in Ceylon and its Extensions."

(a) formal changes in the structure of the pantheon.

(b) the "rationalization" of the cults associated with the worship of gods and demons.

In the cults of the *devas* (gods) practiced in the city, a conspicuous feature is the remarkable rise of one major deity in the traditional pantheon—Skanda—at the expense of practically every other deity. The cult of Skanda is so popular today and it is possible that he will eventually displace all other *devas* in the pantheon. I believe one can relate the ascendancy of Skanda to the rise and spread of the new urban elite described by Wriggins, Ames and Singer. The choice of Skanda as the predominant deity is also interesting, because none of the Buddhist texts, even the late ones, mention Skanda at all. The life of Skanda, a son of Siva, is depicted in the Hindu text, the *Skanda Purana*. Here he is depicted as a powerful god, the slayer of the *asuras* (the enemies of the gods). In the Sinhalese Buddhist pantheon he is not viewed as Hindu, but Buddhist; what is remarkable however, is the *choice* of Skanda as the leading deity for Buddhist urbanites and intellectuals at the expense of deities like Vishnu, to whom according to myth was given the task of protecting Buddhism in Ceylon, and Nata who is viewed as the future Buddha Maitriya. I shall sum up the importance of Skanda for the urban elite in the following manner. Since he is the most powerful of deities in the traditional pantheon—the slayer of the *asuras*—he is viewed as capable of assisting the worshipper to overcome the most difficult of mundane problems. With the rise of the new elite many difficult problems have emerged —problems pertaining to status aspiration, success in business ventures, and politics. Skanda, it is believed, can give the worshipper success, and he is preeminently the deity of the upwardly mobile man—the businessman and the politician, the student studying for his examinations, the bureaucrat waiting for his promotion. His power is so great that even Protestants and Catholics propitiate him. Practically every person going abroad on a scholarship visits the main shrine of Skanda in Kataragama, South Ceylon, to seek his aid for success and safe return. Political leaders of all parties make vows to him for victory at the elections, and motorcades, of both right and left wing, go from Colombo to Kataragama to seek the help of the vanquisher of the *asuras*. Let us illustrate with an example the typical *political* use of Skanda. It should however be remembered that the political use of Skanda, is one aspect of his larger social uses brought about by the kind of problems that a rapidly changing society is facing.

I refer to a political pamphlet written in Sinhalese entitled "How Sirima's Government Fell" (63 pages). "Sirima's Government" refers to the left-wing coalition government of Mrs. Sirima Bandaranaike, incumbent Prime Minister. The Government fell in December 1964, when the Leader of the House, Mr. C. P. de Silva crossed over to the Opposition with thirteen other M.Ps. The author of the tract, a journalist, states that the fall of Mrs. Bandaranaike's government was entirely due to the intervention of Skanda. The sequence of events according to him was as follows.

(a) The God Skanda in a dream told the writer, a former supporter of Mrs. Bandaranaike, to start an opposition newspaper entitled *Vinivida* ("The Piercer"); the "piercer" presumably refers to the golden arrow of Skanda.

(b) The god mustered enlightened public opinion through the medium of this newspaper, cautioning the people against the evils of dictatorship, the "red Chinese menace," corruption and nepotism.

(c) The author promised the God several offerings and *pujas* if he broke "Sirima's Government."

(d) The author was aware that the left coalition were also imploring the aid of the same deity, but he says, the deity scorned the coalition government. Before forming her left wing coalition, Mrs. Bandaranaike, according to the author, consulted a female spirit medium. Skanda, through the medium, had encouraged the then Prime Minister (Mrs. Bandaranaike) to form the coalition government. But, says the author triumphantly, Skanda had deliberately got a mean spirit to utter the benediction, because he (the God) knew that if the coalition was formed Mrs. Bandaranaike's government would fall! "The whole assembly of Gods asked God Skanda to wield his sword and finish the whole business," so unpopular was Mrs. Bandaranaike with the deities. But Mrs. Bandaranaike thought otherwise because for a period Radio Ceylon started their programme with a *puja* for Skanda, hoping thereby to win people over to the coalition point of view. But Skanda was unimpressed because the sound waves of Radio Ceylon penetrates into "unclean and filthy nooks and corners," says the author.

(e) On December 3rd, 1964, the Government fell. It is worth quoting the author in full.

> The Great Powerful Deity residing in the great *devale* (temple) made his kill with his golden arrow. The flaying is now left for our masses. You should pray that God Skanda achieve future Buddahood and do your duty to your country. On the third of December Sirima's Government fell. On that day the leader of the Opposition Mr. Dudley Senanayake (the present Prime Minister) and Mr. C. P. de Silva, the leader of the House (the present Minister of Lands and Irrigation) with a group of M. Ps. visited straightaway the Skanda temple at Bambalapitiya. I was there already from dawn performing *pujas* and breaking two thousand coconuts, till Sirima's government fell. . . .

The God Skanda, slayer of *asuras*, was responsible for foiling a red Chinese plot, for preventing a dictatorship and for the preservation of democracy!

Along with the choice of Skanda as the major deity for urban Buddhists is the rise of the demon of sorcery (*kodivana*) known as *Huniyan Yaka*. According to the traditional pantheon he was a demon (*yaka*); the myth of his ancestry,

the "impure" foods offered to him suggest his inferior status.[34] In traditional
rituals of counter-sorcery he is tricked, cajoled, threatened and banished from
the patient possessed by him. On the urban level the anxieties concerning sorcery
exist; the cognitive belief in sorcery as a causative factor in human misfortune
also exists. But the older ritual technology is being displaced; new temples
(*devale*) and more "dignified" rituals for Huniyan are emerging in the cities.
Moreover his status in the pantheon is different; he is no longer a *yaka* (demon)
but a *devata* (a higher class of supernatural being). The cognitive belief in
sorcery and the personal anxieties associated with it are as dominant on the urban
level as on the peasant. But a rationalization of the cult has occurred. The "vul-
garity" of the peasant ritual has been elided and the status of the deity elevated.

The implications of the preceding analysis are important for they seem to
contradict a common sense assumption that with the increased emphasis on doctrinal Buddhism there must be a concomitant decrease in what Ames would call
"magical-animism" and the placation of *devas*. My contention is precisely the
opposite. Firstly, with the increased "frustrations" due to political and social
change, traditional deities, selectively chosen, are used to overcome these frustrations. Indeed their projected capacities to alter events—e.g., to make and break
governments—are of magnitude rarely paralleled in traditional belief. This however only indicates the magnitude of the modern situation as against the traditional. Secondly, doctrinal Buddhism we noted had few of the accoutrements of
mass religiosity. If so, with an increased doctrinal emphasis there must also occur
on the level of behaviour (howbeit "urban" or "educated") a greater reliance
on magic and astrology. There is a cognitive reordering of these beliefs so as to
make them fit the urban ethos. This cognitive reordering of traditional belief
I shall call the *rationalization* of the religious life.

We have only depicted the ongoing process of cognitive reordering, not its
stabilized final form. Rationalization occurs on two levels. Firstly, there is an
increased emphasis on the doctrinal corpus; Ames has highlighted this nicely.
The behavioural correlative of this increased doctrinal emphasis is a this-worldly
asceticism directed towards political, social and religious goals. If the emphasis
is on doctrine one would expect logically a devaluation of the worship of *devas*;
for the exaggerated intercessionary powers attributed to the *devas* by the urban
elite contradicts the doctrinal assertion that these *devas* have no power. They,
like humans, are themselves *karma* bound. This logically expectable attitude is
found among a few *virtuosi* among the urbanites, who, like Anagarika Dharmapala and the cases quoted by Ames scorn the *devas*. Yet contrary to logical expectation, the *devas* are practically universally believed in by the urbanites, with
a seriousness never seen in traditional peasant worship. This trend is an index
of the enormous frustrations and personal anxieties among the urbanites. There
is an interesting change also on the level of social action. In urban Ceylon there
is an increasing community worship of the Buddha: the worship of the *devas* by
contrast is highly individual. This is almost a reversal of peasant trends where

---

[34] Paul Wirz, *Exorcism and the Art of Healing in Ceylon*, Leiden, Brill, 1954.

group propitiation of the *devas* and the individual worship of the Buddha was more common. This change on the action level is not surprising: Buddhist doctrinal values provide the focus of national unity; whereas the placation of the *devas* is to resolve the frustrations whether social structurally or personally engendered—via the individual. The worship of the Buddha is a public affair: the worship of the *deva* is private.

The rationalization of the religious life on the urban level poses several problems. The resurrection of the Buddhist *doctrinal* values poses few cognitive problems, and follows pretty much the pattern of other world religions facing the impact of modern science and technology. There is a de-mythologizing of peasant beliefs, e.g., the *jatakas*, or birth stories, were myths to the peasant whereas they are fables that point a moral to the urbanite. There are attempts by university dons and intellectuals to advance "proofs" for the "existence" of *karma*, and an attempt to reconcile Buddhism with science. But this is not easy with astrology, magic and the propitiation of *devas*. Peasant magical practices are being increasingly substituted by the recital of Buddhist texts called *parittas* by monks; the notion is that the very recital of the texts banishes evil spirits and brings blessings on householders. But what about astrology and propitiation of *devas?* One rationalization has occurred—worship is elided of the elaborate paraphernalia of peasant ritual with their music, dance, song, prescribed obscenities. Simple *pujas* (rituals) have been substituted. The traditional song and music associated with *deva* and demon worship is now displaced into the worship of the Buddha in an innovation known as "Buddhist carols." These songs are called *bhakti-gi* (devotional songs) self-consciously modelled on the lines of the Christmas carols. The traditional prayers to the Buddha were highly formalized *pali gathas* devoid of song. By contrast *bhakti-gi* are devotional songs with musical accompaniment. The element of song and music traditionally associated with the "lower cults" are now transferred into the context of Buddha worship. The "model" is once again Christian, but the adoption of the model by Buddhists is necessitated by the changes that have occurred in urban Ceylon.

CONCLUSION

The position I have adopted does not imply that these indicators of change are unique to our period in history. Earlier periods of our history, when confronted with similar historical events, may have produced concomitant changes of a similar nature in the religious system. For example, in times of national crisis monks had come into the forefront of events, and had moved out after the crisis was over. At other times, when monks had become too world-involved, reform movements had occurred to check them. However, the scale and intensity of the socio-political changes that have occurred in contemporary Ceylon find no parallel in any one period of our history; concomitantly the changes in the religious orientations of the people are of a previously unparalleled scale. One result of these changes is concentration of power in the hands of the Sinhalese speaking Buddhists. Sinhalese is the official language, and Buddhism, for all practical purposes, the official religion. These changes could not have taken place without the involvement of Buddhists in the affairs of the world. The problem of the paper was: what was the nature of this involvement, and what changes and innovations in the religious system, on both symbolic and action levels have occurred as a result? We have examined the following indicators of change:

(a) Spatial shifts symbolizing the entry of Buddhism into the "world."

(b) Emergence of a leader who provides a charter for change, a model for emulation and becomes a symbol of a new order.

(c) Role shifts, specifically a this-worldly asceticism directed to political and social goals.

(d) Finally a rationalization of the religious life. The last involves a paradox owing to the unique nature of Buddhism. There is a revival of the doctrinal corpus but the Buddha though worshipped, has no intercessionary role and cannot help humans, unlike a monotheistic or any other deity. Hence, deities from the doctrinally unsanctioned "lower cults" are selectively used to assist the worshipper to overcome the enormously complicated problems a changing society is confronted with.

Sinhalese Buddhism and the Dilemmas of Reinterpretation

BARDWELL L. SMITH

In reference to the Ceylonese Buddhist *Mahāvaṃsa* Wilhelm Geiger made the important comment that a study of it "shows us how fallacious it is entirely to separate Buddhism from Brahmanism."[1] While the differences between them are major, not to mention the diversity within each tradition, Geiger's point is instructive for many reasons. *First*, it orients one immediately to the religious point of origin, the Brahmanical tradition, over against which early Buddhism emerged and grew. *Second*, it is a reminder of the sociopolitical framework authenticated by Brahmanism, providing the context upon which the *Saṅgha* and its lay members depended in numberless ways. *Third*, ingredients of its mythology, its art forms, its rituals and even of its caste system become indelibly fused with the Buddhism of *Laṅkā* (Ceylon), whose identity is unimaginable apart from this tradition. *Fourth*, it keeps vivid the constant influence and threat represented by Tamil culture and Tamil invaders throughout most of Sinhalese history. *Fifth*, it is inevitably close to the surface in modern Ceylon which wrestles painfully with the problems of its diverse population, whose Indian minority can neither be wished away by repatriation nor absorbed by conversion. And, *finally*, it is in relationship to India as a nation, whose culture and politics have influenced most of Southeast Asia as well, that Ceylon's future intimately rests.

While the magnitude of these interconnections resembles Indra's Net in scope, only a few aspects bear mentioning in this context. The task at hand is to assess the capacity of contemporary Theravada Buddhism, glimpsed mainly in Sinhalese guise, to abet the process of modernization. "Can religion, which served to legitimize relatively static traditional structures (political, social, economic), be reinterpreted to provide positive ideological support and legitimacy to the modernizing task which is widely understood to be the prime responsibility of the political system? Can reformulated religion become an affective ally of a state committed to extensive socioeconomic change?"[2] Such a task begs a number of questions which will have to be explored throughout this essay, though the main effort will be to phrase the problem in various ways and to suggest dilem-

---

[1] Wilhelm Geiger, *Culture of Ceylon in Mediaeval Times* (Wiesbaden: Otto Harrassowitz, 1960), p. 176.

[2] Donald Eugene Smith, *Religion and Political Development* (Boston: Little, Brown and Company, 1970), p. 201.

mas and possibilities regarding the complexities of Theravada Buddhism and the present social context.

One of the more clear definitions of the modernization process depicts it as being "fundamentally one of differentiation, by which integralist sacral societies governed by religiopolitical systems are being transformed into pluralist desacralized societies directly by greatly expanded secular politics."[3] As a definition, this is a helpful assessment of a process evolving at different rates in different settings. Substantially, this asserts that men can and must plan their societies for the welfare and education of their members and develop relationships in a world community which are mutually constructive. Ideally, it is a concept of politics which combines concern for the total well-being of each person with the awareness that governments are not only fallible but should be limited. A great deal could obviously be said about how this does or does not work in practice, but the task here is to examine the role of Sinhalese Buddhism within the modernizing process in Ceylon.

The particular variants of this problem have important historical and contemporary features which are necessarily related. To discuss modern structural and ideological components of any religious tradition apart from its development over centuries invites distortion. While no picture of Sinhalese Buddhism can serve Theravada at large, there are various features which have suggestive implications elsewhere. The topics selected are six-fold: *one*, the nature of sacro-political authority as perceivable from the classical to the modern period in India and Ceylon; *two*, the beginnings of reinterpretation of certain forms of lay Buddhism with special emphasis upon its social implications; *three*, the nature and impact of Sinhalese Buddhist identity in ancient and current forms, in relationship to *Urbuddhismus* (that perceived essence of the early community) and to the continuing quest for national self-consciousness; *four*, the Buddhist Sangha, its genius for creativity as well as endurance, its patterns of decay and reform, and its present organizational crisis; *five*, the ongoing search for unity in the midst of pluralistic forces, within the Sangha, within the *Buddha Sāsana* itself and within diverse local, national and wider settings; and *six*, the primary vocation of Buddhism, as with every religious tradition, of keeping distinct yet continually relating the two domains, inadequately labelled sacred and profane, encountered by each person and community.

I. SACRO-POLITICAL AUTHORITY

In his analysis of *Kingship and Community in Early India* Charles Drekmeier writes that "a central theme of Indian political speculation is the relationship

---

[3] *Ibid.*, p. 1. Cf. Lucian W. Pye, *Politics, Personality, and Nation Building* (New Haven: Yale University Press, 1962), p. xv, in which he identifies this process as the diffusion of a world culture whose ingredients include "the secular state and the industrialized organization of human activities, the reliance upon rational and conscious choice and a faith in impartial justice, and the acceptance of the virtue of merit and of rewards according to skill."

between brahman legitimation and kshatriya authority."[4] While the legitimation-authority tension in Buddhism differs markedly from the normative Indian prototype, brahmanic assumptions appropriated by the early Buddhist community gave rise to functional counterparts within the Sangha-monarch relationship in Theravada. Basic to this development was the sensed interdependence between power, authority and legitimacy, in which "authority introduces the idea of 'right,' the legitimate use of power."[5] Within the brahmanic tradition there is a rich intermingling of normative and pragmatic approaches to governance, providing a note of realism alongside the canonical standards by which political activity is judged. "Indian culture thus provided the tradition of divine kingship, but it gave also a tradition of purely secular statecraft which freed the ruler from all eventual restrictions resulting from divine kingship—a dualism which must be considered to understand state-Sangha relations."[6]

It is clear from the Ceylonese chronicles that the kings of Ceylon were as versed in the science of statecraft, depicted in the *Arthaśāstra* of Kautalya and conveyed by Brahmin priests within the court, as in the prescriptions for righteousness stemming from both Hindu and Buddhist scripture and custom. This apparent dualism sustained an attitude of ambivalence toward political authority which remains as important now as at the outset of Buddhism. A proper awareness of its significance helps rectify certain fallacious images of Buddhism, let alone Hinduism, as being ahistorical by nature or as having little concern for socioeconomic conditions. In attempting to adjust these images, some interpreters suggest that both constitutional democracy and welfare state socialism were anticipated in original Buddhism. While these adjustments are no less fallacious, it is pertinent here to identify the types of concern about the social order which are preserved in the records.

It is not surprising that the early Buddhist community, being a minority, should have felt somewhat differently about the power of the monarch than their brahmanic counterparts. Buddhist concern at this point goes beyond this expected anxiety, however, questioning the very essence of power in a world of impermanence and self-seeking. In an article on the subject B. G. Gokhale outlines three distinct attitudes which emerged in the first centuries of Buddhist presence in India. "Although the early Buddhists betray feelings of disquiet,

---

[4] Charles Drekmeier, *Kingship and Community in Early India* (Stanford: Stanford University Press, 1962), p. 6.

[5] *Ibid.*, pp. 252-253. Cf. also p. 10: "Hindu political thought never escapes from this dilemma of royal power [*danda*] and priestly authority. The *rajadharma*, the dharma of the king, exists as guarantor of the whole social structure. Danda is thus means, dharma the end."

[6] Heinz Bechert, "Theravāda Buddhist Sangha: Some General Observations on Historical and Political Factors in its Development," *Journal of Asian Studies*, vol. XXIX (1970), p. 766. This statement by Bechert is appropriately qualified by a comment of B. G. Gokhale on the differences between the early Buddhist political thinking and the concepts of Kautalya. Cf. Balkrishna G. Gokhale, "Early Buddhist Kingship," *Journal of Asian Studies*, vol. XXVI (1966).

bordering on fear, about the nature and functions of kingship as it existed in their times, they see no alternative to it and declare it to be absolutely essential to prevent humanity from lapsing into a state of anarchy. Finally, confronted with the fact of kingship and the absolute necessity for it for orderly human existence, they attempt to tame absolute political power by infusing into it a spirit of higher morality."[7]

It is this apprehension about chaos which makes kingly power not only a less threatening alternative but a stabilizing influence as well, conducive to an atmosphere in which men may search for order and meaning beyond and within the order of society. Many recent interpreters of Theravada (among them Gokhale, Mus, Sarkisyanz, Wijesekera and Rahula) have noted an accompanying concern amongst early Buddhists and their successors for the social and economic well-being of all citizens.[8] Not that the Buddha or his followers were social reformers, but that pursuit of the Dhamma depended no less upon adequate economic welfare of the society at large than on stabilized political order. While similar ambivalence toward material goods existed in theory as toward power, the Sangha realized its own dependence upon the liberality of others as well as the threat to order represented by widespread privation. "Ideally kingship had, therefore, to guarantee such economic relationships as would ensure a sufficient livelihood for its subjects—to allow them the leisure for meditation on which depended the achievement of Nirvana."[9] In correcting the impression of Max Weber that no social ethics were derivable from Theravada, Sarkisyanz appropriately distinguishes between what he calls the ethos of lay Buddhism and the ethos of the Buddhist order of monks, yet stressing the bridge that exists "between this 'Arhat' ideal and active social endeavor."[10] It would be a mistake either to see no connection between them or to miss the radical disjunction. The supreme tension was suggested first by the Buddhist monarch Asoka who, in explaining what lay behind his welfare measures, said, "I have done what I have primarily in order that the people may follow the path of Dharma with faith and devo-

[7] Gokhale, op. cit., p. 15. Gokhale adds the following statement: "In this line of reasoning, then, the state is never an end in itself but rather a means to an end. As an instrument, it is possessed of total power that encompasses within its jurisdiction all areas of human activity. It is an awesome power and it is per se neither moral nor immoral. But it cannot exist outside of human beings for it is not just an abstraction or a thought-construct; it can be exercised only through human agencies. It is this association of total power with human beings that creates the dilemma of power. Orderly human existence is not possible without power but power is easily misused and often is misused. The Buddhists set themselves to find an answer to this problem of total power." Cf. p. 20.

[8] Cf. also Drekmeier, op. cit., p. 255: "The king's chief duty was, of course, to protect his subjects. But this involved more than law enforcement. By the fourth century B.C. there had been a notable increase in the welfare functions of the state in India. . . . If the sacred tradition was upheld, the country would prosper; this idea had the effect of making the king accountable for the general prosperity of the people as well as for their security."

[9] E. Sarkisyanz, Buddhist Background of the Burmese Revolution (The Hague: Martinus Nijhoff, 1965), p. 56.

[10] Ibid., pp. 36-37.

tion."[11] While claiming no special merit for his policies, he underscored the motivation behind them. Whether one reads such statements cynically or accepts them at face value, one finds in Asoka the *locus classicus* of kingly prudence and virtue, a man whose own violence had been converted into justice, *ahiṃsā*, and righteousness. The miracle to later Buddhists, as recorded in the legends about Asoka (*Aśokāvadāna*), was that statecraft could be imbued with virtue, a belief which led them to term him *dhammarājā* and to second Asoka's own belief that *Dhammavijaya* (conquest through righteousness—i.e., over attachment and ignorance) was possible.

The model of the ideal king, however, is done little service if one neglects in the reading of Sinhalese and Burmese history the continuing reappearance of cunning, violence and self-assertion amongst kings and others. While the chronicles of both nations are clearly *Heilsgeschichte*, heavily didactive in nature, they attest with extraordinary honesty to man's capacity for evil. The corruption of power, the misuse of authority and the illegitimate exercise of kingship described in the records highlight the fragile yet essential relationship between legitimation and authority. In the person of kings whose exercise of power is tamed, either by the tenderness of their own conscience or by sanctions of the Sangha whose political power lay in accessibility to popular support, we find a remarkable interdependence or at least, in political terms, a balance of power.

There have been many accounts of how this symbiosis benefitted the Sangha itself.[12] The *Mahāvaṃsa* records the extensiveness of kingly patronage, the monarch's role in settling disputes within the *bhikkhu* community, and the delicate yet crucial task of initiating reform (*sodhesi sāsanam*) within the Sangha whenever indiscipline or heresy became issues. While one would expect the portrayal of centuries to include pictures of lawless monks and treacherous kings, the chronicles are also replete with testimonies about how power in fact was tamed.[13] Such kings become in deed and word *Sāsana Dāyakas*, that is, protectors and promotors of the faith, models not simply for other monarchs but for all men.

Unless the contemporary Sinhalese Buddhist scene is portrayed against this historical and ideological background, one comprehends inadequately the process

[11] N. A. Nikam and Richard McKeon, eds. and trs., *The Edicts of Asoka* (Chicago: University of Chicago Press, 1959), p. 65.

[12] Walpola Rahula, *History of Buddhism in Ceylon* (Colombo: M. D. Gunasena and Co., second edition, 1966). Cf. p. 70: "The influence of the Saṅgha over the masses was so great that rulers were careful to win the hearts of the bhikkhus for the sake of peaceful and successful government. To obtain approval of the Saṅgha was to ensure public support." Cf. also Balkrishna Govind Gokhale, "The Early Buddhist View of the State," *Journal of the American Oriental Society*, vol. 89 (1969), pp. 737-738. Also S. Arasaratnam, *Ceylon* (Englewood Cliffs: Prentice Hall, Inc., 1964), pp. 78-79. Also, Geiger, *op. cit.*, pp. 203-215; Rahula, *op. cit.*, *in passim*; Arasaratnam, *op. cit.*, pp. 80-81; and Richard A. Gard, "Buddhism and Political Authority," in Harold D. Lasswell and Harlan Cleveland, eds., *The Ethic of Power: The Interplay of Religion, Philosophy, and Politics* (New York: Harper and Brothers, 1962), pp. 43-48, 55-58.

[13] Wilhelm Geiger, tr., *The Mahāvaṃsa* (London: Luzac and Company, Ltd., 1964). Cf. p. 245 for a typical passage.

of introspection and renewal occurring within this tradition. Wherever one ex-
amines the picture within the past hundred years, one may observe laymen and
bhikkhus wrestling with the fact that the former sacro-political authority was no
more. Some blame this upon the British for "dishonoring" their agreement,
under the Kandyan Convention of 1815, to uphold the Buddhist religion. Some
trace it to the beginnings of colonialism under the Portuguese in 1505; some to
the decline of the Sinhalese civilization itself, starting in the thirteenth century.

What cannot be denied is that Sinhalese Buddhism, as every religious tradition, now confronts a world in which entirely different assumptions, having
social and political and economic implications, are operative. If past assumptions
were diverse, though relatively stable, present ones are bewilderingly complex
and in constant flux. If the task for religious institutions and their membership
were simply to apply old teachings to new situations, the dilemma would be real
enough. Instead, they are confronted with what is essentially a religious task,
namely, the question of identity, in an age where the tension between sacred and
secular is shattered or unperceived, or where the sacred is allowed one room in a
mansion seen as secular. As one analyst put it: "The attack on traditional systems took various forms and moved at varying speeds, but everywhere it cracked
open the integralist nature of society. Everywhere it separated the major components of the religiopolitical system. Religion could no longer legitimize political power in the convincing way it once had done, nor could governments confi-
dently arrange ecclesiastical affairs in the traditional manner. The disruption of
traditional systems left governments without legitimacy and autonomous religions with no prior experience of autonomy.' "[14]

II. THE BEGINNINGS OF REINTERPRETATION*

It is clear that changes in religious thinking, behavior and organizational
structure are intimately related to shifting patterns within the culture at large.
This is nowhere more evident than in the reexamination beginning to take place
within traditionally oriented religious systems in areas of rapid social change, as
elsewhere. It is equally apparent that various forms of Buddhist reinterpretation
now visible are in direct continuity with socioeconomic developments occurring
throughout modern life. While more conservative Buddhist elements blame colonialism for destroying the traditional role of the Sangha (in many ways this
charge is accurate), there is increasing willingness amongst certain Buddhists to
favor within institutional Buddhism itself reformulations along certain lines.

If some of the changes are primarily tactical in the effort to cope more effectively with a highly complex modern society, others are more fundamental.
While reform of the Sangha has taken place periodically throughout Buddhist
history, there is growing realization that monastic divisions, whether caste-based

[14] Smith, *op. cit.*, p. 10.

*This section is a revision of pages 210-213 of an article by the author, "Toward a
Buddhist Anthropology: The Problem of the Secular," *Journal of the American Academy
of Religion*, vol. xxxvi (1968), 203-216.

or sectarian in nature, detract from the Sangha's impact upon lay society.[15] Even more basic, and bound ultimately to effect organizational patterns, is the developing recognition of the layman's role within Theravada, an affirmation which has been looked upon with ambivalence in the Sangha, though the upgrading of the layman has taken place with a minimum of friction thus far, for a number of reasons: first, no effort has been made to abolish the monastic institution; second, a genuine attempt has been forthcoming throughout Theravada to universalize an ethic of "ascetic pietism" and not to disparage renunciation; and third, a sense of frustration has become widespread among educated laymen themselves about how Buddhism can relate effectively to modern society.[16] The present concern about modern institutional life has certain unprecedented aspects. Behind it lies an awareness of how inadequate have been the efforts "to mediate between the perfectionist demands of the classical canon and the hard, perplexing choices that individual laymen must face each day in a society that is very different from the Buddha's."[17] Should the pressures for this mediation become stronger, they are bound to create new images of reality and new patterns of authority within the Buddhist community.

Disappearing rapidly are the days when the Five Precepts (*Pañca-sīla*) for laymen are considered adequate guides for ethical behavior. Disappearing also are the days when the monastic community by itself can designate authoritatively the meaning of being a Buddhist in society. In fact, the days may be gone when responsible Buddhist life in the world is seen as less difficult than withdrawal to a hermitage. While no blurring of the distinction between these stations need occur, indeed no disparaging of either one, a more balanced complementarity between them may be emerging. It is a moot question whether the increased importance of the layman is responsible for certain doctrinal changes, or whether changing emphases within doctrine provide the impetus for the "new layman." In all likelihood, both elements derive from a vastly different historical situation wherein greater proportions of laymen than ever are moving into the middle

---

[15] Cf. B. H. Farmer, "The Social Basis of Nationalism in Ceylon," *The Journal of Asian Studies*, XXIV (May, 1965), pp. 437-438; Cf. W. Howard Wriggins, *Ceylon: Dilemmas of a New Nation* (Princeton: Princeton University Press, 1960), pp. 191-198. The activity of the All-Ceylon Buddhist Congress, the Sri Lanka Maha Sangha Sabha, the Eksath Bhikkhu Peramuna (United Bhikkhu Front), and other organizations that took shape before and during the 1956 campaign provide evidence at this point. So too does the attempt by U Nu and the Clean Anti-Fascist People's Freedom League in Burma during the late 1950's.

[16] On the growth of meditation centers for laymen in Ceylon, cf. Michael M. Ames, "Ideological and Social Change in Ceylon," *Human Organization* XXII, (Spring, 1963), p. 51; also for the same development within Burma, cf. Winston L. King, "New Forces in an Old Culture," *The Antioch Review*, XXI (Summer, 1961), pp. 163-164. The growth of such centers may hold both promise and danger for Buddhism in the modern day— promise, in helping to deepen the spiritual life of lay devotees; danger, in serving to palliate, rather than understand creatively, the problems of society.

[17] Wriggins, *op. cit.*, p. 193.

class with its educational accompaniment. This development will lead to others, in doctrine as well as in the centers of influence in the Buddhist community.

Doctrinal reinterpretation is becoming another area of Buddhist reassessment within the current scene. About the nature of this reinterpretation, no clear consensus exists within Theravada. On the other hand, a "certain directionality" is apparent,[18] three elements of which should be mentioned here. The *first* is the suggested compatibility of *Nibbāna* as the ultimate goal of life and as discoverable in history, within the social order. Nibbana in the latter sense is conceived not as limited to a remote future or as something other-worldly. While never far from the danger of so liberalizing the concept as to make it indistinguishable from the "worldly," some stress the need to discover Nibbana "here and now," or at least to begin to discover it here and now. In Walpola Rahula's words, "he who has realized the Truth, Nirvāṇa . . . lives fully in the present."[19] As growing number of Buddhists are looking upon Nibbana as open to laymen as well as monks, so the first fruits of Nibbana may be experienced within the framework of present existence itself.

A *second* and related element is the conceived coexistence of tranquillity (*upekkhā*) with compassion (*karuṇā*). Within this are various sub-elements. One is the interpretation of upekkha to mean not "detached neutrality" or "negative uninvolvement" but equanimity through non-attachment, not through non-involvement. Another is the insistence that the doctrine of *kamma*, properly understood, leads not to fatalism but to greater awareness of human responsibility and human freedom. Another is the appropriation of the *bodhisattva* concept as fundamental to all Buddhism, not just within Mahayana. Buddhists who favor these doctrinal interpretations still claim that detachment and renunciation are necessary steps, but assert that the result is more positive in connotation, i.e., that the tranquillity discoverable through non-attachment is far from neutral in its impact upon the world and results rather in increased compassion and unique involvement with the needs of men.

A *third* element combines continued respect for traditional Buddhism with an unmistakable drive for reformulations of doctrine, organization and practice. There is a gradual shift, among laymen especially, away from accepting certain traditional formulations to a disposition that is more pragmatic and exploratory by nature. This is, of course, what Buddhist modernists have stressed repeatedly about their religion, namely, its rationality and scientific bent. If these claims are somewhat ambiguous, there is little doubt about the new questioning of authority. Fundamental here is not simply the conviction that Buddhism can speak effectively to the modern world, but even more that Buddhists must explore new areas of thought and involvement. As yet this realization has borne little fruit,

---

[18] Cf. especially King, *op. cit.*, pp. 158-162; Ames, *op. cit.*, pp. 48-50; also, Winston L. King, *In the Hope of Nibbana* (La Salle, Illinois: Open Court Publishing Co., 1964), pp. 226-236.

[19] Walpola Rahula, *What the Buddha Taught* (New York: Grove Press, Inc., 1962), p. 43.

but it is unquestionably part of the present mood.[20] In such a context a new sort of Sinhalese Buddhist identity is being formed.

III. SINHALESE BUDDHIST IDENTITY

The manner in which a community in times of profound crisis reaches into the past to discover its identity and redefine itself in relationship to this past, even to perceive distinction and uniqueness over against it, has considerable psychological and social importance. Frantz Fanon captures the essence of what has been occurring in a global sense during the past generation: "In order to ensure his salvation and to escape from the supremacy of the white man's culture, the native feels the need to turn backward towards his unknown roots and to lose himself at whatever cost in his own barbarous people."[21] The humiliation of colonial status, the emergence into an incompletely prepared for freedom, and the accelerating of a pace which destroys faster than it reconstructs[22] breed insecurity and fear which not unsurprisingly issue in self-assertiveness, sometimes in hatred, often in further confusion about identity. While hardly limited to transitional societies, the dilemmas attendant to national self-discovery are especially poignant in these contexts.

> There is no doubt that nationalism has proven a potent force for national integration and for developing a new sense of purpose, helping to sweep away the anxieties and uncertainties resulting from the nation's shifting identity. In fact, the preoccupation with national identity itself is an inherent part of nationalism. The insistence on the uniqueness of one's own nation has occasionally, however, also led to the glorification of attitudes and values that were integral parts of the value system of the closed agricultural society from which it is emerging. Although the reconfirmation and elevation into permanent virtues of these values and attitudes undoubtedly contribute to greater self-confidence, they may at times make creative adjustment to the needs of modernization more difficult by prematurely freezing or fixing the self-image into a somewhat traditional cast.[23]

Attention has frequently been drawn to the involvement of Buddhist monks in anti-colonial movements specifically, but the ingredients of nationalist senti-

---

[20] One of the most candid expressions of this is the following: "To bring about this transformation the Sangha must be reorganized and the bhikkhus trained not only in Buddhist theory but also in some form of Social Service in order that they may acquire a personal knowledge of practical problems. Thus they would live in closer touch with humanity, would better understand and sympathize with human difficulties, and would exert their influence as much in living as in preaching." Cf. D. C. Vijayavardhana, *The Revolt in the Temple* (Colombo: Sinha Publications, 1953), p. 586. This advice is diametrically opposed to that of the well-known sectarian movement in Ceylon, the Vinaya Vardhana, which wants to remove monks from society altogether.

[21] Frantz Fanon, *The Damned of the Earth* (New York: Grove Press, Inc., 1964), p. 175.

[22] Pye, *op. cit.*, p. 12.

[23] Soedjatmoko, "Cultural Motivations to Progress: The 'Exterior' and the 'Interior' Views," in Robert N. Bellah, ed., *Religion and Progress in Modern Asia* (New York: The Free Press, 1965), p. 5.

ments in Ceylon need exploring if Sinhalese Buddhism's impact upon future social change is to be foreseen in any sense. Heinz Bechert accurately observes that
a critical study of the Ceylonese chronicles "reveals the part played by the political concept of the national identity of the Sinhalese in close connection with the
religious tradition of Theravada Buddhism, i.e., the concept of the identity of
the Sinhalese Buddhists."[24] The continuity of modern Sinhalese nationalism with
its classical counterparts since the third century B.C. is too important to go un-
mentioned. National and religious self-consciousness have been identified since
that time, normally in moderate, occasionally in virulent, form.

The national crisis of May 23-27, 1958 which issued in communal riots between Sinhalese and Tamils, killing several hundreds and requiring the declara-
tion of a state of emergency, was only the most recent major episode of violence
between these two communities which, while co-existing within Ceylon in reasonable toleration of each other until modern times, also have a history of antipathy dating back to ancient times. "The fact that the threat came mainly from the
Tamil kingdoms across the straits served to keep alive the vision of the Tamils
as the enemy of the Sinhalese people. . . . Thus it was that a people who had
very close cultural relations with each other were cast politically in the role of
antagonists."[25] While more recent forms of antagonism have stemmed principally from economic and social considerations (i.e., from the sizeable Tamil
immigrant labor force used in plantation estates and from the relatively higher
proportion of Tamils in civil service positions and in commerce), the resultant
communalism has carried racial and religious overtones which only compound
the other real problems. Most symbolic of all has been the debate, during the
middle and late 1950's especially, over the question of national language, as language and cultural identity can scarcely be separated.

To understand the dilemma presently felt by Sinhalese Buddhists, not to
mention Tamils, it is helpful to perceive how their current crisis of identity had
earlier manifestations and to relate current and historical forms to the claims both
of their own uniqueness and of their uninterrupted continuity with the original
Dhamma. These twin claims are clearly opposite sides of the same coin and serve
to establish their unique destiny as primary recipient and conveyor of what the
Buddha taught. The legitimation of their own future and of changes occurring
within it depends in no small measure upon their ability to reinterpret the meaning of their past identity, in a religious sense.

---

[24] Bechert, op. cit. Cf. also Richard H. Robinson, The Buddhist Religion: A Historical Introduction (Belmont, California: Dickenson Publishing Company, Inc., 1970),
p. 115: "Everywhere, Buddhists have been staunch nationalists, have taken part in anti-
colonial movements, have claimed to be custodians of the national culture, and have longed
to reestablish the old symbiosis between Sangha and state. In a secular age, this dream is
not going to come true, but nationalist sentiment will undoubtedly maintain Buddhism
wherever freedom of religion prevails. However, the Dharma is presently too weak, and
the Sangha, too dependent, to exercise moral authority and restrain political excesses. Most
citizens are nationalists first, and Buddhists second, if at all."

[25] Arasaratnam, op. cit., p. 60. King Duttugemmu (Duṭṭha-Gāmiṇī) reigned 161-
137 B.C.

In his depiction of the agonies faced by key figures in post-independence Burmese political and administrative echelons, Lucian Pye sketched the vicious circle which "seems to develop in transitional societies: fears of failure in the adventure of nation building create deep anxieties, which tend to inhibit effective action; thus imagined problems become real and fears of failure become the realities of failure; and these failures further heighten anxieties."[26] As an ingredient of this, Pye underscored the deep-seated apprehension about chaos, the phobia of uncontrollable emotions, of running amok. "A latent fear of anarchy and a suspicion that all people must be controlled against dangerous and aggressive impulses are basic elements in Burmese political thought."[27] While peculiar forces within Burmese society help to account for this, the phenomenon is discoverable in various forms in all societies. The recurring necessity of dealing with forces of disorder within and between men tend to blur the psychic and spiritual differences between so-called traditional, transitional and modernized societies. The reversion to chaos is no respecter of time or place. A combined critical and sympathetic reading of the Ceylonese chronicles, juxtaposed against the events of more recent times, provides insight into the Sinhalese quest for identity and its implications for the future.

Lanka's self-image of being the "archetype of delusion" and the "paragon of enlightenment" reinforced her vocation as upholder of the Dhamma's purity, injecting into Sinhalese identity a comparable insistence upon national purity. In the modern day, *Dhammadīpa* (the island of the teaching) embarks upon exorcism of foreign elements, whether Christian influences from the colonial era or the Westernization of its urban elite or all languages but Sinhala only or, through repatriation plans, several hundred thousand Tamils.[28] While advocated primarily by extremists, large sections of the population were caught up in a renewed search for their Sinhalese self-consciousness. The preparations for the Buddha Jayanti (1956) and the installation of the first Buddhist governor general (1962) were both symptom and capstone, ceremonially, of this quest.

It is the very uncertainty about identity which drives a community to expel all elements from its presence which dilute its desired purity, yet it is paradoxically in relationship to differences within one's midst that a more secure identity can be forged. It may not be an inappropriate interpretation of history to say that one of the factors helping to produce a creative and distinctive Sinhalese civilization was the very presence of Tamils, upon the island and across the straits, throughout the centuries. As frequently observed about Roman Catholicism, it is precisely in those situations where the Church has not had a monopoly, so to speak, that it has been most alive and the least doctrinaire. Comparably, it may not be untrue about Sinhalese Buddhism that part of its fortune has ironic-

---

[26] Pye, *op. cit.*, p. xv.

[27] *Ibid.*, p. 106. Cf. also pp. 139-141.

[28] Heinz Bechert, *Buddhismus, Staat und Gesellschaft in den Ländern des Theravāda-Buddhismus* (Frankfut am Main und Berlin: Alfred Metzner Verlag, 1966), Band I, pp. 112-114.

ally been in having this Tamil thorn in the flesh. While the classic encounter between Duttugemunu and Elara, the Tamil king of Ceylon, restored the monarchy to Sinhalese Buddhist hands and marked the beginnings of Sinhalese nationalism, it could not still the fears that political chaos and the forces of *adhamma* were ever-present. The centuries separating the monk Buddharakkhita's complicity in the 1959 assassination of Prime Minister S. W. R. D. Bandaranaike from the assurance given by eight arahants to Duttugemunu who was distressed over slaughtering Elara's "great host numbering millions" were symbolically spanned.[29]

One additional aspect of Sinhalese Buddhist identity requires noting here, namely, the indissoluble connection with its Indian roots. The very mention of the Buddha himself, Vijaya, Asoka, Mahinda and Buddhaghosa attests to Sinhalese dependence upon its continental forebears. The continuance of apostolic succession (*ācariyaparamparā*) from Upali in the Buddha's time to Mahinda and beyond, the implication of Sakka and innumerable named and unnamed brahmanic deities in the many paradigmatic events of early Sinhalese culture,[30] and the involvement of Brahmin priests in coronation ceremonies (*abhiseka*) of Buddhist kings further suggest how both orthodox and *volksreligion* elements of the Hindu tradition became merged with Sinhalese self-consciousness. Without question, the ambivalence toward things Indian needs resolving if temptations toward communalism are not to harden still more. Sinhalese Buddhist identity suffers no loss by acknowledging its brahmanic heritage, while still legitimately claiming it had chosen a different path. In which case, Tamils too might relax. The creative wrestling with religious self-awareness carries crucial import for social and political developments in the future. Lucian Pye has put the challenge as follows: "Fundamentally, the hope for transitional peoples resides in their quests for new collective as well as individual identities. Their development hinges on their capacity to find meaning in a fusion of what we have called traditional and modern modes of action, a fusion of world culture and their own historic cultures."[31] There is no culture to which these words do not apply.

[29] *Mahāvaṃsa*, p. 178. This assurance confirmed the faith of Duttugemunu who earlier had gone forth to battle with the cry, "not for the kingdom but for the doctrine [Buddhism]." Cf. also Rahula, *History of Buddhism in Ceylon*, pp. 228-229, for the incongruous endorsement of violence by arahants.

[30] E.g., the consecrating of Vijaya, the arrival of the relics, the coming of the Bodhitree, the enshrining of the relics, et al. Cf. Wriggins, *op. cit.*, pp. 239-240: "Despite this cultural heritage many Sinhalese are keenly sensitive to the ebb and flow in their own creative energies. More than five centuries separated the late Polonnaruwa period from its predecessors and another five hundred years intervened before the Kandyan kingdom put its stamp on the culture of the central highlands. The coming of the Europeans, it is felt, all but destroyed many aspects of indigenous culture. Many Sinhalese, therefore, consider their culture fragile, requiring unusual defenses if it is to survive in proximity to the vigorous Tamil culture and in the face of insistent European influences."

[31] Pye, *op. cit.*, p. 287.

IV. THE SANGHA: ORGANIZATIONAL CRISIS

If Theravada Buddhism has typically thrived on state support, we may be on the verge of seeing developments within Theravada having no precedent. While still the case in Cambodia and Thailand that the Sangha relates to the state in a traditional manner, this is no longer true in Burma and Ceylon and, in the long run, the former instances may prove anachronistic. Though the history of British colonialism took different turns in Ceylon than Burma, in both the state's connection with Buddhism became severed. It is no wonder that members of the Buddha Sasana felt confused, betrayed and irate with the loss of patron, defender and arbitrator. If the symbiosis had not been without its trials, in theory and frequently in fact the state's role as Sasana Dayaka was crucial for the Sangha. Without speculating on what this dislocation meant for the state, for the Sangha the word crisis is none too strong. While the nature of the crisis is varied, its principal element is organizational. Donald Smith phrased it well: "Buddhism today is faced by serious problems of internal organization. Under the conditions of modern life, religion can function effectively only if organized coherently so that it can transmit its teaching to each new generation, protect its collective interests, and exert its moral influence on society and government. In Buddhism the laity is not organized into effective local units, the problem of indiscipline within the Sangha is very serious, and there is only the most tenuous connection between the laity and the Sangha."[32]

In order to grasp what role the Sangha may play as legitimator of change in the future, it is essential to examine certain components of this organizational crisis, for without structural and ideological coherence there can neither be significant legitimizing nor critique of change. Among many components, five will be identified here: the problem of organizational unity in a situation composed of immense fragmentation; the ongoing question of discipline within the bhikkhu community; the ironic but not unprecedented tension between the vow of poverty and monastic affluence; the dilemma of advancing to the laity more responsibility and influence without detracting from the Sangha; and, finally, the largely unexamined matter of maintaining a sensitive balance between what Heinz Bechert calls *Urbuddhismus* and *traditionalistischen Buddhismus*.

1. At the heart of the problems affecting Sinhalese Buddhism today is the question of reform. There is no issue of importance to either the internal life of the Sangha, the relationship between bhikkhus and laymen, or the impact of Buddhism upon contemporary thought and society which is not centrally dependent upon how and in what ways reform takes place. Inevitably hinging upon reform is the matter of organizational coherence, the problem of unity. On the surface, the rejection by the Sangha of major reform measures suggested by the Buddha Sasana Commission in its 1959 Report was due to their having become a political football. Beneath the surface, however, it was clear that what was being recom-

---

[32] Donald Eugene Smith, *Religion and Politics in Burma* (Princeton: Princeton University Press, 1965), p. 327.

mended was a totally new ecclesiastical polity, one which would reconstitute the operation of institutional Buddhism. Fundamental to these recommendations was the establishment of a bicameral deliberative body called the Buddha Sasana Mandalaya, to be composed of two councils—one, of bhikkhus from all three *nikāyas* or sects, responsible only for internal matters within the Sangha; the other, of both bhikkhus and laymen, "which would undertake to promote the general welfare of the Buddhists, meet the challenge to Buddhism from opposing forces, and deal with the state in regard to the rights of the Buddhists."[33]

There have been many accounts of why these efforts failed.[34] In essence, the Sangha obviously felt threatened; the disunity within the Buddhist community which the Report sought to remedy was transcended only by uniform rejection of its measures. In fairness to the Sangha it cannot be said that what was being rejected was the state's right to reform and purify the community. This right had been confirmed, by custom, at least from the time of Asoka.[35] It would be more true to say that an attitude of trust had yet to be created toward a completely new kind of constitutional polity. To exist in interdependency with a Buddhist monarch is one thing; to entrust one's destiny in major ways to an untested conciliar body is quite another, particularly when it meant that state-Buddhism was being rejected forever as a matter of policy.

On the other hand, the necessity of devising some sort of organizational clarity and corporate responsiveness to a host of human needs would be denied by few in Ceylon today. The extraordinary involvement of bhikkhus and laymen in social and political activity during the past two decades bespeaks of immense vitality, but the requirement for greater effectiveness appears even clearer. "The direct involvement of larger sections of the Sangha in political affairs in Ceylon as well as Burma in recent times was connected with an important change of its organizational structure, namely, the emergence of monks' associations outside the traditional structures of the nikayas. . . . As a result, a new form of dualism in the life of the Sangha came into existence: for monastic and religious matters one had to stick to the traditional nikaya structures—for political and social activity the bhikkhus joined associations with no connection at all to the nikaya

---

[33] C. D. S. Siriwardene, "Buddhist Reorganization in Ceylon," in Donald E. Smith, ed., *South Asian Politics and Religion* (Princeton: Princeton University Press, 1966), p. 545. He continues: "It was to undertake the traditional functions of the Buddhist king in promoting the general welfare of Buddhism and also take upon itself the functions appropriate to a religious organization in modern society."

[34] Cf. Bechert, *op. cit.*, Band I, pp. 267-285; Wriggins, *op. cit.*, pp. 195-201; Smith, *South Asian Politics and Religion*, pp. 460-467, 500-509. Cf. also his analysis of somewhat comparable problems in Burma in *Religion and Politics in Burma*, pp. 186-229. Cf. also Rahula's account of sectarian developments in ancient Ceylon, *op. cit.*, pp. 194-197, *inter alia*.

[35] *The Edicts of Asoka*, pp. 67-68: "The monk or nun who disrupts the Saṁgha shall be required to put on white robes [instead of the customary yellow] and to live in nonresidence (*anabasasi*). It is my desire that the Saṁgha be united and endure forever."

organization."[36] If the pyramidal system of the bhikkhu community in Thailand, with a Supreme Patriarch (Saṅgharāja) at the head and an elaborate infrastructure as part of it, is not acceptable in either Burma or Ceylon, some sort of functional equivalent will need to be developed.

2. No less dependent upon sasana reform is the issue of discipline. While organizational restructuring may be prior logically, the very problem of indiscipline, coupled with the disappearance of state involvement in these matters, may become the primary catalyst toward establishing ecclesiastical tribunals, which were also part of the Buddha Sasana Commission Report. To create jurisdictional bodies of this sort, however, without giving serious attention to Vinaya reform and the vocation of the bhikkhu in the light of present needs is to miss central opportunities, even to betray Buddhism. The debates about reinterpreting the Vinaya date back at least to the Second Council (at Vaiśālī, 377 B.C.), leading to the emergence of the Mahasanghikas and other sectarian developments later. As Rahula put it, "the Vinaya was not ultimate truth, but only a convention agreed upon for the smooth conduct of a particular community."[37]

The *symptoms* of indiscipline reveal themselves in bhikkhu laxity of behavior, partisan political activity, occasional acts of violence, monastic landlordism, even sectarianism; the *substance* of indiscipline goes far deeper. It relates inevitably to the vocation of the Sangha as preserver of the Dhamma, besides which all its activities are subsidiary. The qualitative distance between the average monk or layman and the Buddha or the great exemplars through history cannot be measured in terms of centuries. To use the Vinaya as anything but means toward this qualitative goal is, indeed, a betrayal of Buddhism. This is not to stress disproportionately Buddhism's social message,[38] which must derive from renewed quality of life within; it is only to distinguish substance from form, end from means.

[36] Bechert, "The Theravāda Buddhist Sangha," *op. cit.*, pp. 777-778. This article is a helpful portrayal of sasana reform historically and in different Theravada settings. It also deals with the issue of structure in relationship to this.

[37] As he says, a critical study of the *Vinaya Piṭaka* shows "how the original rules were modified by supplementary regulations to meet new situations." Cf. Rahula, *op. cit.*, pp. 153-154. Technically, the rules were not changed, only reinterpreted, but in practice they amounted to changes. Cf. also Robinson, *op. cit.*, pp. 42-45. While these interpretations would not be shared by most bhikkhus today, they are not inconsistent with the counsel and practice of the Buddha.

[38] The most influential single example of this over-emphasis is probably *The Revolt in the Temple* which sees Buddhism primarily as a social gospel. Heinz Bechert's treatment of Buddhist modernism analyzes several of the same tendencies during the past hundred years in Ceylon and elsewhere. Cf. Band I, *op. cit.*, pp. 36-108. While the modernist movement has many emphases (e.g., rationality, accord with scientific principles, support of lay activity, counter-colonialism, organizational restructuring of Buddhism, the international Buddhist movement, scholarship in Buddhist materials, general educational improvement, et al.), one of its purposes was the creation of an effective social ethic. For Buddhism to relate significantly to the modern world this will be necessary; on the other hand, it cannot be seen as the substance of Buddhism.

The sense of alarm and the cries for reform proceeding from public response to Sinhalese bhikkhu political activity in the late fifties were not only a response to excessive behavior, they were expressions of disenchantment and confusion about what a true bhikkhu should be. Without knowing it, these were not dissimilar to comparisons made by the Buddha. With a nice ironic touch, in sayings later called the *Brāhmanavaggo* (or, *Way of the Brahmin*), Gautama defined the model bhikkhu in terms which that age could comprehend: "Him I call a Brahmin who is without hostility among those who are hostile, who is peaceful among those with uplifted staves, who is unattached among those who are attached.... Him I call a Brahmin whose wisdom is deep, who possesses knowledge, who discerns the right way and the wrong and who has attained the highest end."[39] Though descriptive of an ideal, the ideal had worldly implications, some of which will be discussed in the final section. Here it only need be said that the Sangha must emancipate itself from dependence upon external stimuli alone for reform. While remaining sensitive to these stimuli, authentic reform must proceed from within, though that is precisely the problem.

3. The necessity of new structures are not only to handle problems of disunity and indiscipline. "There is need also for organization to deal with the material needs of the Sangha. In the old village units the support and maintenance of the monks was a duty readily undertaken by all Buddhists. . . . However, the village no longer depends on the temple as it did in the past, and the bonds of interdependence have almost disappeared. . . . Unless the laity are able to ensure conditions that will enable the 'bhikkhus' to live strict lives, it is useless to expect purity in the Sangha, and it is foolish to blame the monks for these violations of the Vinaya."[40] The problems, however, are less simple than they sound; as with the other two instances, a long history lies behind them. In fact, much of Ceylon's social history is involved with monastic temporalia and their administration. With the British period, separation of land from the Sangha began. The Colebrook Reforms of 1832-34 and the enforcement of the 1856 Temple Land Registration Act during the years 1857-65 were the most prominent steps taken.

The primary anomaly is not extensive ownership of land by the Sangha but that it is principally held by up-country elements dominated by the Siam Nikaya, the largest and wealthiest of the three nikayas in Ceylon,[41] and that most temples on the island are marginally supported at best. This is not the place to discuss the complexities (legal, ecclesiastical, fiscal) of the situation but only to identify

---

[39] S. Radhakrishnan, tr., *The Dhammapada* (London: Oxford University Press, 1966), p. 183, verses 24 and 21 respectively. For a description of the attitude of people in ancient Ceylon toward impurity within the Sangha, see Rahula, *op. cit.*, p. 259.

[40] Siriwardene, *op. cit.*, p. 544.

[41] Wriggins, *op. cit.*, pp. 191-192. Cf. Bechert, Band I, pp. 225-244, for a thorough description of this situation. Cf. also his article on the Sangha, mentioned earlier, in which he discusses an instance of successful sasana reform in East Bengal, in which the monks are "in a certain sense under the control of laymen" and where reform was successful "not in spite of the poverty, but on account of the poverty of their monastic institutions."

this among the more serious issues within the general organizatonal crisis of the Sangha, one which clearly complicates, if not compromises, its ability to address itself effectively to other social and political concerns.

Siriwardene is correct, nevertheless, in pointing out that guaranteed means of support must be found if the Sangha is to fulfil its basic vocation. Neither attachment to affluence nor the threat of involuntary poverty are conducive to spiritual uplift or influence upon society. The dilemma, of course, is both how this support can be forthcoming from non-governmental sources or, if from the government, how it can be justified within a secular state concept. If funds are given to Buddhists, then Tamils, Christians and Muslims will expect support too. With Ceylon's marginal economy, there is little to spare, though one measure might be a guaranteed minimal income for all citizens. Whatever the solution, the problem for the Sangha is considerable, as with any monastic community where the vow of poverty competes with the generosity of pious laymen, not to mention the diligent use of these gifts by clerical hands.

4. The fourth problem is also the greatest opportunity, namely, the relationship between bhikkhu and layman and the need to reconceive this relationship in such a manner that neither be diminished and both gain. In a traditional sense, the same kind of reciprocity existed between monk and laity as between king and Sangha, the latter in fact being the prototype for the former. Whatever distinctions existed among laymen and among monks, the final dividing line *between* them was that "acquiring merit of various kinds was the motive underlying the religion of the laity, from the king down to the poor peasant," while monks were expected to tread the path to Nibbana.[42] The term *dhamma-dāna* expresses vividly the nature of the reciprocity, i.e., the giving of "spiritual, cultural and educational gifts" in return for material ones.[43]

Whatever can be said about the continuation of this pattern in urban areas, as well as in the villages, a social and a cultural revolution has been occurring which has begun to effect considerable changes. Not only the secularizing process, but the upgrading of education produces a population as sophisticated in most respects as their clerical counterparts. This makes available increasing numbers of people who can serve the Buddha Sasana and society in general in new ways. Their role in education, in organizational activities, in "ecumenical" Buddhism, and even in Buddhist studies has already been immense. In fact, if not in theory, the role of the laity has undergone its own revolution. What is called for is a reconceived doctrine of the layman, plus his inclusion in decision-making councils at local and national levels, enabling his service to be expressed in more thoughtful and responsible ways.

The consignment of laymen to less than equal partnership was understandable in a traditionalist framework, but it will prove self-defeating if continued. Because of the continuing tendency in all religious traditions for false distinc-

---

[42] Rahula, *op. cit.*, p. 252. Cf. pp. 251-262 for further description of monk-lay attitudes toward each other. Also, Robinson, *op. cit.*, pp. 47-49.

[43] *Ibid.*, p. 194.

tions to exist between lay and clerical members, there is often an attempt made by laymen to become diluted versions of ministers, priests, or monks and to conceive morality in narrow and often puritanical forms. What results is a version of religious thought and behavior which in no significant way analyzes, confronts or transforms the culture. Consequently, secularism in its most distorted forms goes unchallenged and the process of secularization as a legitimate enterprise is afforded no profound religious guidance. For laymen to be given a vision of what real service to their fellow men through their loyalty to the Buddha Sasana can mean, an entire transformation of perspective is required.

Finally, it is no inconsistency to say that in the process renewed dignity must be given to the monk, as his is a role the layman cannot serve and which society clearly needs. Distinctions do exist between them but these are of training, role, function and opportunity—not necessarily of dedication, compassion or wisdom. The latter distinctions do exist among men and Buddhism has a name for those who have attained high levels of spiritual growth (*sāvaka-sangha*), but it is always stressed that this community of attainment is a spiritual one (i.e., supra-empirical) and is not restricted to monastic disciples of the Buddha.[44]

5. In both Burma and Ceylon the shift from a negative anti-colonialism to a more positive ideology created a vacuum into which rushed a resurgent but not reformed Buddhism. "Post-independence nationalism had to be nurtured on something which was both positive and indigenous."[45] The correspondence between national self-consciousness and the renascence of indigenous cultural forms is a world-wide phenomenon. Earlier, we noted the present Sinhalese Buddhist attempt to rediscover dimensions of self-identity which had been stifled or ignored in recent experience. A similar development, in slightly less complex form, can be traced in Burma, in the person of U Nu and others. It is generally characteristic of enduring religious traditions that they accommodate themselves to changing times and circumstances, absorbing and transforming various elements to which their members are exposed. The history of Buddhism reveals that its aptitude here is excelled by none.

This does not mean either that the appropriation of indigenous beliefs, art forms, practices or structures is indiscriminate or that important distinctions are

---

[44] Cf. Donald K. Swearer, "Lay Buddhism and the Buddhist Revival in Ceylon," *Journal of the American Academy of Religion*, vol. xxxviii (1970) and Gananath Obeyesekere, "Religious Symbolism and Political Change in Ceylon," *Modern Ceylon Studies*, vol. 1 (1970), reprinted in Chapter Three of this volume. The latter has a particularly interesting section on Dharmapala (1864-1933) in which the author stresses the meaning of the *anagārika* role which Dharmapala assumed and included in his new name. "Anagārika" means "homeless" and symbolizes, Obeyesekere suggests, the combination of the monastic renunciation with worldly involvement, a kind of this-worldly asceticism in the Calvinist sense, fitting neither the pattern of the typical monk nor typical layman. Dharmapala was other than both, yet he sought to combine the advantages of each in a way unprecedented within Sinhalese Buddhism.

[45] Smith, *Burma*, p. 120.

not retained between local and indigenous on the one hand and orthodox or traditional on the other. In its Theravada modes especially, Buddhism maintains these distinctions carefully. Anthropological studies of locales in Thailand, Burma and Ceylon are virtually unanimous in describing a basically two-tiered system, often with more precise refinements, of indigenous folk religious expression superimposed by more or less canonical Theravada.[46]

What has happened during the past twenty years in Burma and Ceylon is that political capital has been made of indigenous religion, of folk-Buddhism and of orthodox Theravada, with the assistance of elements within the Sangha, by candidates seeking to ingratiate themselves with the rural masses and the more sophisticated. The vital new ingredient in the picture is that through universal suffrage Buddhism becomes politicized in unprecedented ways, not infrequently resulting in disorder and communal violence. Here too, as with the four issues discussed above, the dilemma is compounded by the organizational crisis within Sinhalese Buddhism. What is called for is a sensitive distinguishing of *Urbuddhismus* from its cultural expressions, without either demeaning or glorifying the latter. This is as much an organizational problem as an intellectual one, since until the members of the Sangha are provided educational opportunities comparable to the laity they cannot fully participate in the process. While there is obvious risk in this venture, there is ultimately more to gain than to lose.

V. OUT OF PLURALISM, UNITY

When the sun finally set on the British Empire, Westernized elites in places like Burma and Ceylon found themselves face to face with their own people. In Ceylon, unlike Burma, there had not been the kind of struggle for independence which tends to weld together differences within a population, so that national consciousness begins to transcend communal differences. With the advent of universal adult franchise, through the Donoughmore Constitution of 1931, the active politicization of communal elements within the society became a possibility. In 1956, this possibility was actualized, making Ceylonese politics since that time bitterly partisan along religious lines. This problem of antipathy between Tamils and Buddhists, if not between Buddhists and Christians, had been foreseen by the royal commissioners who visited the island in 1927-28 in preparation for the 1931 constitution. Their report proved prescient, though their approved recommendation that representatives be chosen on regional, not communal, bases did not prevent increased discord. "Not only is the population not homogenous, but the diverse elements of which it is composed distrust and suspect each other. It is almost true to say that the conception of patriotism in Ceylon is as much racial as national and that the best interests of the country are

[46] Cf. Manning Nash, ed., *Anthropological Studies in Theravada Buddhism* (New Haven, Southeast Asia Studies, 1966). Cf., also Ediriweera R. Sarachandra, "Traditional Values and the Modernization of a Buddhist Society: The Case of Ceylon," in Bellah, *op. cit.*, for a sensitive plea for Sinhalese Buddhism to integrate folk culture with the higher culture of the traditional elite.

at times regarded as synonymous with the welfare of a particular section of its people."[47]

The functional-valuational pluralism which develops through secularization is, by definition, not yet achieved in societies moving from traditional to modern patterns. In fact, it is often true of the transitional stage that its simultaneous appeals to the past and the future are unbearably strained. And also, where a society is diverse religiously, "the appeal to religious identity may prove severely disruptive to nationalism or may lead to the development of regionalist or separatist subnationalisms."[48] It was precisely this appeal in the mid-fifties which opened up old wounds in the Ceylonese body politic. This price political and religious leaders seemed willing to risk in exchange for popular support and legitimation through the polls, though they were unable to contain the bitterness once released. It will be one of the tests of Sinhalese Buddhist ability in the future to advance and legitimate constructive change without appealing to narrow communal interests.

The task, of course, is not for Buddhists alone, nor even primarily for religious groups. The task must be accomplished through effective political and economic means, though it may be obstructed or abetted by temple, church and mosque. Perhaps the single most important present assignment for religious communities in Ceylon and elsewhere is to legitimate the change from narrow to inclusive definitions of human identity, in policy as well as creed. In essence, this will mean the secularization of group identity, which may paradoxically release religious communities to serve in new ways. Both Burma and Ceylon are presently in mid-stream in the effort to achieve a new national self-consciousness which integrates substantive values from their traditions with the development of a modern nation state. "The diverse demands and values of each group must in some measure be drawn into the political process, if large numbers are not to be in fact alienated from the political order."[49] The skills which are called for are immense—political, administrative, scientific, educational, industrial, economic, legal, among others. The temptation to substitute charisma and rhetoric, however sincere, for competence is never absent. The example of U Nu in Burma provides a grim reminder both of how religious legitimacy can be misused and of how sectarian and separatist elements in a pluralist society thrive on politically promoted religion. The understandable fears of minority groups in such situations (e.g., Christian Karens in Burma and Hindu Tamils in Ceylon) not infrequently trigger potential secession movements, as Ne Win's March 2, 1962 *coup* to arrest this movement in Burma and as the Federal Party in Ceylon would indicate.

---

[47] Government of Ceylon, *Report of the Special Commission on the Ceylon Constitution* (Colombo, 1928), p. 31. Cf. Wriggins, *op. cit.*, pp. 211-270, for an excellent chapter entitled "The Problem of National Unity."

[48] Bellah, *op. cit.*, p. 219. Cf. also, Donald Smith, *Religion and Political Development*, pp. 10-12, 241-245, for a discussion of the movement toward a functional-valuational pluralism.

[49] Wriggins, *op. cit.*, p. 50.

The need to develop adequate pressure group channels, effective yet flexible party discipline, and a network of other organizations (political, economic and social) to serve as infrastructure between the state and the society at large is transparent if the various sectors of the community are to feel represented and part of a larger whole. Besides, a number of studies on Ceylon have indicated the economic factors behind communalism, which inevitably are translated into political form. Part of the task of diversifying the economy, which is essential to the island's welfare, is to make available training and vocational opportunities on an open basis. The very clustering of ethnic groups in certain areas of the economy and the perjorative attitudes toward various kinds of work perpetuate stereotypes Tamils and Sinhalese already have of each other. If religious institutions are to participate significantly in this process of changed attitudes and changed relationships through a reconstruction of organizational patterns and options, there is need for considerable reflection about which means best serve the goal of an open society. Donald Smith has stated it succinctly: "The most effective ideological reformulations, then, would be those which (1) evolve out of extensive multilateral ideological interaction, (2) are authenticated by established ecclesiastical authority, (3) are transmitted by a well-organized communications network, and (4) are associated with meaningful action programs."[50] Obviously, each context must create its own ways of meeting these criteria for the responsible legitimation of change.

Intrinsic to a religious community's serving the political and social goal or fashioning constructive unity out of pluralistic elements are its own efforts to blend unity and diversity within itself and in relationship to other religious traditions. While this is a task for all religions within a society, there is a special onus which falls upon those in the majority. The tensions between elements within the Sangha, the "tenuous" connection between bhikkhu and layman, the deep-lying hostilities between Christians and Buddhists (as well as between Buddhists and Tamils), and the lack of continually significant interchange with those who are hostile or indifferent toward religious values are obviously key items on the agenda in Ceylon, as everywhere in their varying forms. Thus far, it is more common for defensiveness and counter-attack to dominate the exchanges than graciousness, though there are many examples to the contrary. What has been said about Indian nationalism applies, with appropriate changes, to its Sinhalese counterpart, namely, that it will not be secure if it "equates [Buddhist] glory with [Hindu] humiliation."[51]

One important development on the world scene which is bound to influence Sinhalese Buddhism considerably in the long run, more than it already has, is the movement of international or "ecumenical" Buddhism. This is another instance of cultivating unity out of diversity. While part of the Mahayana canon, it is

<hr />

[50] Smith, *op. cit.*, pp. 203-204.

[51] Selig S. Harrison, "Hindu Society and the State," in K. H. Silvert, ed., *Expectant Peoples: Nationalism and Development* (New York: Random House, 1963), p. 299. Harrison's phrase was "Hindu glory with Muslim humiliation."

well-known that the *Lotus Sutra* talks about *ekayāna*, or one vehicle rather than two. It is this which some Theravada Buddhists are talking about today and which does not promote homogenization of Buddhism, let alone false syncretism with aspects of other religions, but a oneness of spirit enabling persons who prefer to retain their differences to be open toward each other. "Basically, the question for world-wide Buddhism today is how to harmonize the various facets of Buddhism —the memory of Gautama Buddha, the authority of the canonical writings, the nebulous but real power of tradition, and the living experience of men and women in their particular cultural and historic situations."[52] The harmonizing of the ingredients within Buddhism inevitably relates to the existence of harmony between men, Buddhists and others, a harmony which honors differences of belief and practice but strives for oneness of spirit. That most politically astute of Buddhists (Asoka), whose orthodoxy may not have been impeccable yet whose spirit of tolerance has often been noted, put it as follows: "King Priyadarśī honors men of all faiths, members of religious orders and laymen alike, with gifts and various marks of esteem. Yet he does not value either gifts or honor as much as growth in the qualities essential to men in all faiths. . . . The objective of these measures is the promotion of each man's particular faith and the glorification of the Dharma."[53]

VI. TWO DOMAINS IN TENSION

The important sentence in the above-quoted Edict of Asoka is the final one, in which the intent of all his policies is made clear. What he says about tolerance fits into that larger context. Tolerance is never an end in itself. Without it, men become closed to each other, but settling for tolerance alone prevents further growth of mind or spirit. As intolerance produces radical disjunctions where communication might exist, so overtolerance sees accommodations where these are inappropriate. The Dharma, which Asoka sought to glorify, has helped the Buddha Sasana through centuries maintain a balanced perspective, not simply about two domains of life but more about two ways of looking at all existence. Examining these helps to suggest (hopefully without doing violence to the tradition) how Theravada Buddhist conceptualization could make the transition, in its thinking about the political order especially, from a framework presupposing an integralist sacral society to one both pluralist and secular. This endeavor is obviously heuristic in nature, not prophetic.

In his several writings on the early Buddhist views of kingship, the state, and history B. G. Gokhale has elaborated this theory of two domains or of "two 'wheels,' two distinct realms of action" within the dominion of "two separate but equally important ideals of a *Cakkavatti*, the leader of the temporal realm, and

---

[52] Joseph M. Kitagawa, "The Buddhist Transformation in Japan," *History of Religions*, vol. 4 (1965), p. 336.

[53] *The Edicts of Asoka*, pp. 51-52.

the *Bodhisattva*, pre-eminent in the spiritual domain."[54] These domains are intended to reinforce each other, the state as protector and the Sangha as conscience of the state. "Affairs of this world and those of the next are like two wheels. Each has its own distinct identity but they are also like the wheels of the chariot, the axle on which they revolve, in this case, being the human society, its desires, aspirations and destiny. There is also the implication that *Dhamma* cannot operate in this world by itself as it needs the acquiescence, if not support, of *āṇā* or the state. The state and Order are separate in their own identities, but their interdependence cannot be ignored completely."[55]

To stop there would take us no further than the symbiosis described in section one. In another context, however, Gokhale comments that "Buddhism views reality on two levels, ultimate and proximate or transcendental and phenomenal (*pramaṭṭha* and *sammuti*)."[56] It is this distinction, not one between "this life" and "the next life," which makes the substantive point. Clearly, Hinduism and Buddhism do talk about the next life; the whole theory of karma presupposes successive incarnations until one is released from *saṃsāra*. The implication here, on the other hand, is both a qualitative distinction between ways of viewing reality (this life *or* the next life) *and* an assertion that one therefore actually sees different reality as one's state of consciousness deepens. To regard the domains mentioned above only in terms of state and Sangha (temporal and spiritual, even secular and sacred) is to treat superficially what is actually profound. Terms like "sacred" and "secular" become reified, with some things or ideas or institutions ending up in one category and some in the other.

It is not incidental that in later Indian Mahayana there was a deliberate merging of the two distinct but overlapping notions of sovereignty—one, of the sociopolitical; the other, of the cosmos at large. Paradoxically, the original choice of vocations put before the infant Siddhattha was later viewed as a false dichotomy, for as the Universal Ruler or Ideal King is also the Cakkavatti or Bodhisattva, so the Buddha is supreme monarch, the master of heaven and earth. What is implied is not a political but a spiritual sacralization, in which one who is fully enlightened sees the oneness in all reality. He sees the *dhammatā* or "principle of order that makes the world a cosmos and not a chaos."[57] This is comparable to what Edward Conze has said about Dharma, that "although it is the unconditioned One, it is not some barren remoteness, but infuses order into the

---

[54] Gokhale, "Early Buddhist Kingship," *op. cit.*, p. 22. "The theory of the two domains is well expressed by a putative statement of Ajātasattu (circa 493-462 B.C.) at the commencement of the First Buddhist Council held at Rājagaha when he said to the assembled monks, 'Yours is the authority of the spirit as mine is of power' (*dhammacakka* and *ānācakka*)."

[55] Gokhale, "The Early Buddhist View of the State," *op. cit.*, pp. 732-733.

[56] B. G. Gokhale, "The Theravāda-Buddhist View of History," *Journal of the American Oriental Society*, vol. 85 (1965), p. 356.

[57] *Ibid.*, p. 357.

multiple appearances of the conditioned world, and conformity to it is the basis of the spiritual life."[58]

It is this binary orientation which the Buddhist perspective can help provide the modern world where, despite the questioning of all ideologies, there is as much danger of fragmentation in a pluralist framework as of imposed order in an integralist one. In common with prophetic traditions within the West, there is within Buddhism a fundamental critique of man's attempts to elevate partial truths into absolutes. "The perfection of wisdom consists in the direct realization that all dharmas, whether conditioned or unconditioned, are empty."[59] "The teaching of emptiness [*śūnyatā*] repudiates dualities . . . between the relative and the absolute. It cannot be called monism, however, because it denies that reality is either a plurality or a unity. . . . This doctrine comes to terms with the early Buddhist quandary about the relationship between the nirvana-realm and the world. Not only is nirvana immanent in the world, but neither exists without the other."[60] "Salvation from transmigration is to be found in the process of transmigration itself."[61]

The work of social welfare, even the reconstruction of society along more rational and just lines, is therefore crucial to the nirvanic quest, though not equatable with it. While a need clearly exists for the legitimation of economic development, there is equal need not to define this as the good life. While valuational universalism may be an improvement over what is being displaced, its temptation may be blindness to particularity. Pluralist societies do provide opportunities their predecessors could not offer, but they are no less ambiguous in a qualitative sense. In short, "it is necessary to relate the purposes of the development process to other worthwhile purposes of human endeavor and of society."[62] Only after discussing the involvement of Buddhists in society is it appropriate, perhaps, to acknowledge that the Buddhist goal is a form of freedom to which the ordinary social goals do not point. As a good deal of recent activity on the part of bhikkhus and laymen in Burma and Ceylon would suggest, there is some danger that Buddhism may fall into the trap of equating social revolution with genuine freedom. Again, while this freedom cannot be conceived apart from concern about the total welfare of human beings, the quest for it takes many paths, most of which cannot be seen. At a conference on "Religion and Progress in Modern Asia" held in 1963 Clifford Geertz made some comments which are as appropriate now as then: "There may be an intrinsic tension between the spiritual needs of man and the material needs of man, which can never be completely done away with no matter how clever one is or how much one

[58] Edward Conze, "Dharma as a Spiritual, Social and Cosmic Force," in Paul Kuntz, ed., *The Concept of Order* (Seattle: University of Washington, 1967), p. 240.

[59] Robinson, *op. cit.*, p. 51. The Hindu term *sanātana dharma* (eternal or cosmic law which continually needs to be reinterpreted) is suggestive here as well.

[60] *Ibid.*, pp. 52-53.

[61] *Ibid.*, p. 22.

[62] Soedjatmoko, *op. cit.*, p. 2.

manipulates institutions or anything else. The real problem in any state or in any religious tradition is . . . how to keep these two different things in balance."[63]

CONCLUSION

Equal to the necessity of reexamining its past in new ways is Sinhalese Buddhism's task of confronting an emerging world culture with its diverse yet many common features. As the past one rediscovers is inevitably a mixed picture, so the future will prove no less ambiguous. To exorcise the demons of colonialism, or of anything else, is not to avoid the dilemmas of renewed self-determination. "In such a climate an appeal to a venerable past can no longer be a guarantee of contemporary relevance. One of the effects of this heightened historical consciousness is a keener sense of the relativity of historical phenomena and a certain detachment from those currently occupying the scene."[64] With its stress upon the continuing impermanence of all phenomena, its counsel of detachment toward all gain and loss, and its warnings about how easily attachment issues in possessiveness, fear, self-assertion and suffering, it may be that the Buddhist tradition and its values do in fact promote fewer "dogmatic approaches to politics" than is generally common.[65] If so, these may not only facilitate the adjustment to changes ahead but help shape these very changes.

In this regard, three points are appropriate. First, as Wilfred Cantwell Smith has stressed, false images are sometimes conveyed about open, rapidly changing modern cultures in distinction to rigid, moribund religious traditions. While these images may be dead horses now which few men are beating, there has been a serious underestimating of "the dynamic, fluid quality of the so-called traditional religious systems. . . . If one is going to think in dichotomies at all, the proper picture is more nearly the confluence of two rivers, than the impact of one rushing river on a rock (or mud) citadel."[66] "The case is not simply one of dynamic political processes acting upon static religious traditions."[67]

Secondly, while identifying change with progress is unbuddhistic as well as naive, it does not make one a cynic to disbelieve in progress theories, to regard change itself as ambiguous, or to have considerable reservations about what is "legitimized." Neither need it prevent man from acting, nor from becoming better able to judge what changes may, in fact, improve which situations. In the last analysis, progress is a matter of the spirit, though societies fail here too if they remain unconcerned about the political and economic well-being of their

[63] Clifford Geertz, "Modernization in a Muslim Society: The Indonesian Case," in Bellah, *op. cit.*, pp. 166-167.

[64] *Renew and Create*, p. 20, published by the 36th General Chapter of the American Cassinese Congregation (Benedictines), June, 1969.

[65] Smith, *op. cit.*, p. 198.

[66] Wilfred Cantwell Smith, "Traditional Religions and Modern Culture," unpublished address presented at the XIth Congress of the International Association for the History of Religions, Claremont, California, September 9, 1965, pp. 5-6.

[67] Donald Smith, *op. cit.*, p. 33. Cf. also pp. 201-202.

members. Asoka was not the only Buddhist to take this position; he was simply the most conspicuous political figure within Buddhist spheres of influence to do so.

And, third, for reasons not only of easing the transition from more traditional patterns of social organization to more modern ones, but also to help preserve the essence of historic cultures, it is just as important to emphasize continuity as change. In this regard, if one task of religious communities in years ahead is to legitimate change, there will be need also to cultivate the same heights of personal and social awareness (i.e., modes of cultic anamnesis) characterizing their past at its best, in which what the past discovered may be re-experienced in the present, providing channels for the expression of profound personal and corporate existence. The tension between "ambitions for new forms and tenacious adherence to old practices"[68] must be resolved by sensitive leaders, among others, who "want to modernize their country without destroying the fundamental values of their own traditions, for these are the source of their consciousness of self and their originality."[69]

It is inevitable that emerging cultural forms, like earlier ones, will combine important new insights and values with new prejudices and limitations.[70] This does not demean the best of what is now becoming possible; it simply suggests that balanced legitimation of change is always tentative, never total. As with monarchs of old to whom extraordinary power and authority were granted, their continuing legitimacy was not independent of how these were used. Among the more promising developments upon the modern scene is the manner in which constitutional governments, industrial corporations, educational institutions, and elites within science and elsewhere are being held increasingly accountable by the body politic for the ends they serve and the means they employ. While still unclear what sorts of roles religious values and communities interpreting reality in religious ways will play in this development, it is inconceivable they will be silent or that they will have no influence. In essence, what a religious community must do in order to develop new forms of viability is well put by Robert Bellah:

> It must be able to rephrase its religious symbol system to give meaning to cultural creativity in worldly pursuits. It must be able to channel motivation disciplined through religious obligation into worldly occupations. It must contribute to the development of a solidary and integrated national community, which it seeks neither to dominate nor to divide, although this necessity certainly does not imply sanctioning the nation as a religious ultimate. It must give positive meaning to the long-term process of social development and be able to value it highly as a social goal, again without necessarily taking social progress itself as a religious absolute. It must contribute to the ideal of a responsible and disciplined person. As part of the new balance between religious and secular in modern

---

[68] Pye, *op. cit.*, p. xiii.

[69] Wriggins, *op. cit.*, p. 469.

[70] *Renew and Create, op. cit.*, p. 24. Compare this with the attitude toward change in ancient India or Ceylon, where it was regarded as symptomatic of degeneration. Cf. Rahula, *op. cit.*, pp. 199-205.

society, it must be able to accept its own role as a private voluntary association and recognize that this role is not incompatible with its role as bearer of the society's ultimate values.[71]

Specifically, about the role of Sinhalese Buddhism within the "modernizing" process in Ceylon, one may make the following summary comments:

1. While it strikes one as historically fallacious to assert that early Buddhism was socialistic in any recognizable sense, given the structuring of traditional societies, it may legitimately be claimed that there is nothing in Buddhist doctrine or tradition which necessarily militates against the sharing of wealth or the means of production by socialistic legislation and practice. Indeed, though socialism is no more a guarantee of justice than other economic systems, the goal of distributed wealth is quite consistent with the intent and spirit of early Buddhism, if not its primary interest. It must be added, however, that various forms of monastic landlordism in Ceylon would not be supportive of genuine socialism if this meant the loss of widespread temple holdings.

2. While also true that legitimate assertions cannot be made for the existence of genuine democracy on the national level until recently, despite claims about republican forms of polity during the time of the Buddha, it is plausible to defend Buddhism's strong interest in the welfare of each person and, by extrapolation, to argue that widespread involvement in the political process is conducive to a healthy social order. It must be recognized, however, that this will entail not only a stronger role played by Buddhist laymen but a profoundly reinterpreted position about the relative merits of political, social and economic goals, within the general framework of a Nibbana-centered orientation. Though the compatibility of these is far from impossible, it is not always self-evident.

3. While it would be incorrect to portray historical Buddhism as being free from caste, sectarian, or communalistic elements, despite its tendency to claim the contrary, it has both been able to transcend these in many respects and to engage in significant sasana reform over the centuries. The future impact of laity and Sangha upon significant political and social developments, nevertheless, will be directly related to their ability to overcome major internal divisions and to resist continuing temptations toward communal prejudice and separation. The recent history in Ceylon and Burma is a sobering reminder that old wounds take more than time to heal.

4. Finally, while the beginnings of a fundamentally reinterpreted Buddhism, starting with the modernist movement of the nineteenth century, has often stressed its relationship to the social order (defined vaguely sometimes as Buddhist socialism) and while there has been an immense increase in the political and social activity of Buddhists during the modern period, it remains true that

[71] Robert N. Bellah, "Epilogue: Religion and Progress in Modern Asia," in Bellah, *op. cit.*, p. 202.

the primary goal of Buddhism is not a stable order or a just society but the discovery of genuine freedom (or awakening) by each person. It has never been asserted that the conditions of society are unimportant or unrelated to this more important goal, but it is critical to stress the distinction between what is primary and what is not. For Buddhists to lose this distinction is to transform their tradition into something discontinuous with its original and historic essence. Even the vocation of the bodhisatta is not as social reformer but as the catalyst to personal transformation within society. The central task of Buddhism in the immediate future is to display the reconciliability of what often seem diverging paths.

From Philology to Anthropology:
A Bibliographical Essay on Works Related to
Early, Theravada and Sinhalese Buddhism

FRANK REYNOLDS

During the past one hundred and fifty years literally thousands of books, translations, and articles concerning the closely interlocked but by no means identical traditions of early, Theravada, and Sinhalese Buddhism have appeared in English and other Western languages. In the discussion which follows our purpose is to establish certain guideposts which may facilitate the task of the reader who wishes to utilize this vast range of resources in order to explore more fully some of the themes which have been adumbrated in the preceding essays. In order to accomplish this objective we have chosen to be selective and interpretive, and to focus attention on a relatively small number of publications which, in our judgment, are of special importance and interest.[1] In the first section of our discussion we will refer to some forty items which deal with the ancient Indian background of Buddhism, and with the structure and development of the early tradition. In the second section we will refer to another fifty or so items which concern the Theravada tradition, including among them both secondary interpretations and translations of original texts. And, finally, in the third section we will refer to approximately seventy items which deal with the context, structure, and development of Buddhism in Ceylon.

Certainly anyone who is seriously interested in early Buddhism must take into account the Indian context within which the tradition first emerged and developed into a full fledged religious system. An excellent starting point for those interested in "placing" Buddhism within the Indian context is Damodar Dharmanand Kosambi's book, *Ancient India; A History of Its Culture and Civilization* (New York: Pantheon Books, 1966), which culminates in a discussion of the Mauryan era and the rise of the "universal" religions. Though he writes from an explicitly Marxist perspective Kosambi is by no means doctrinaire, and his discussion is filled with important insights. A second very stimulating discussion, which utilizes both sociological and psychological categories of interpretation, can be found in the "Introduction" and the section on "The Decline of Tribal Culture and the Emergence of the Two Powers" in Charles Drekmeier, *Kingship in Early India* (Stanford, California: Stanford University Press, 1962).[2] A comprehensive treatment, written in a more traditional historio-

---

[1] In making our selections we have given first priority to works which have been published in English. However we have found it necessary to include a number of French and German items which have not been translated and which have no reasonably adequate English equivalents.

[2] Drekmeier's book includes a topically organized bibliography which is extremely useful in pinpointing further sources.

graphic mode, is contained in the volume on *The Age of Imperial Unity* in the *History and Culture of the Indian People* series edited by Ramesh Chandra Majumdar (1st ed.; London: G. Allen and Unwin, 1951). On the other hand, those who are interested in short, concise discussions will find that there are no better sources than J. W. de Jong's article, "The Background of Early Buddhism" in the *Journal of Indian and Buddhist Studies (Tokyo)*, XII, 1 (January 1964), pp. 34-37 and A. L. Basham's "The Rise of Buddhism in its Historical Context," *Journal of Asian Studies* IV, 3 (December 1966), pp. 395-411.[3]

Among the studies focused more explicitly on the way in which the religious, philosophical, and symbolic aspects of the ancient Indian tradition are related to early Buddhism, by far the richest and most provocative are Paul Mus' three hundred page preface to his remarkable *Barabadur: Esquisse d'une histoire du Bouddhisme fondée sur la critique archeologique des texts* (Hanoi: Imp.d'Extrême-Orient, 1935) and his short article, "The Thousand Armed Kannon" which appears in the *Journal of Indian and Buddhist Studies* (Tokyo), XII, 1 (January 1964), pp. 1-33.[4] However he presents his material with such great erudition and in such a convoluted literary style that all but the most determined students must be satisfied with the summary of a few of his important contributions which has been provided by Orlan Lee in an article entitled "From Acts— To Non-action—To Acts: The Dialectical Basis for Social Withdrawal or Commitment in the Buddhist Reformation," *History of Religions Journal*, VI, 4 (May 1967), pp. 273-302. Alongside Lee's essay those interested in the Upanishadic roots of Buddhist concepts should consult Étienne Lamotte and Jean Przyluski, "Bouddhisme et Upanishad," *Bulletin de l'École Française d'Extrême-Orient*, XXXII (1932), pp. 141-169; those interested in the relationship between early Buddhism and yoga should consult Chapter V in Mircea Eliade, *Yoga; Immortality and Freedom* (Princeton: Bollingen Series LVI of Princeton University Press, 1958; now available in paperback edition.); those interested in the immediate intellectual environment should consult A. K. Warder, "On the Relationship Between Early Buddhism and Other Contemporary Systems," *Bulletin of the School of Oriental and African Studies*, XVIII (1965), pp. 43-63; and those interested in comparing early Buddhism and the Bhagavadgita may receive some suggestions from the a-historical and rather polemical essay by K. N. Jayatilleke entitled "Some Aspects of the Bhagavad Gita and Buddhist Ethics," *University of Ceylon Review*, XII, 1 (April-June, 1955), pp. 135-151 and republished in *Aspects of Buddhist Philosophy* (Wheel Publication, Nos. 128/129; Kandy: Buddhist Publication Society, 1969).[5]

[3] Like Drekmeier's discussion, de Jong's article is explicitly in the tradition established by the classic, but now dated treatment of Buddhism in Chapter VI and VII of Max Weber's *Religion of India*, Free Press Paperback (New York and London: The Free Press and Collier-Macmillian Co., 1967).

[4] A listing of important classical works is included in Constantin Regamey, *Buddhistsche Philosophie* (Bibliographische Einführungen in Das Studium der Philosophie, 20/21; Bern: A. Franke, 1950).

[5] Though both interpretations are seriously oversimplified it is worth mentioning that

Though more material has been written on early Buddhism than any of the other topics which will concern us in the present essay, the key items are not difficult to identify. The first few pages of Edward Conze's article on "Recent Progress in Buddhist Studies" in his *Thirty Years of Buddhist Studies* (Columbia, S.C.: University of South Carolina, 1968) provide a much needed antidote for many popular misconceptions concerning early Buddhism; and in addition they present a concise and accurate picture of many of the problems being confronted by contemporary scholars as well as the methods which they are using to deal with them.[6] The most up to date and interesting narrative accounts of the development of the early tradition are found in Sukumar Dutt's *The Buddha and Five After-Centuries* (London: Luzac, 1957) and his *Buddhist Monks and Monasteries of India* (London: G. Allen and Unwin, 1962). Though the former is devoted exclusively to the first five centuries, the discussion of the same period in the opening chapters of the latter is greatly enhanced by the fact that in the interim between the publication of the two works, Dutt had gained a much greater appreciation for the role and contribution of the Buddhist laity. Though it is considerably too academic and detailed for the general reader, Étienne Lamotte's massive *Histoire du Bouddhisme indien, des origines à l'ère Saka* (Louvain: Publications Universities, 1958) constitutes an absolutely essential resource for anyone who intends to carry on a more serious study of the tradition and its development. Lamotte's treatment is extremely comprehensive and erudite, his judgments on disputed problems are always balanced and carefully defended, and his footnotes provide an entrée not only into the whole range of Buddhological literature, but into the original sources as well. And finally, the most exciting and challenging interpretation, which gives full weight to the symbolic and cultic aspects of the tradition, is found in Mus' *Barabadur* (Mus' discussion includes an original and highly suggestive thesis concerning the way in which the Pali and Mahayana traditions emerged from the "common Buddhism" of the earliest period).

Alongside the general studies of early Buddhism there are a number of more particularized works which should also be mentioned. Two rather different but largely complementary discussions of the Founder are available in E. J. Thomas' *The Life of the Buddha as Legend and History* (3rd ed. rev. 1949; reprinted; New York: Barnes and Noble, Inc., 1952) and Alfred Foucher's *The Life of*

---

the typically Hindu view of Buddhism as just another variant of the "perennial philosophy" expressed in the Brahmanic tradition is developed in characteristic form by Ananda Coomaraswamy in the section on "Contemporary Systems" in *Buddha and the Gospel of Buddhism* (New York: G. P. Putnam and Sons, 1916; available now in paperbound edition from Harper Torchbooks), while the somewhat more defensible contention that Brahmanism, with its conception of the Self, and Buddhism, with its emphasis on the doctrine of No-Self, represent two antithetical strains in Indian religious thought is developed by T. R. V. Murti in the first chapter of his *Central Philosophy of Buddhism* (London: G. Allen and Unwin, 1955).

[6] Conze's footnotes provide an excellent bibliographical source for a number of more technical works which were published prior to 1959 when the article itself was written.

the Buddha According to Ancient Texts and Monuments of India, abridged trans. by Simone B. Boas (Middletown, Conn.: Wesleyan University Press, 1963); the former is adequate for introductory purposes, though somewhat dated, while the latter is a more recent treatment which makes effective use of archaeological and iconographic evidence.[7] In addition to these biographical studies Ananda Coomaraswamy's article on "The Origin of the Buddha Image," *The Art Bulletin,* IX 4 (June, 1927), pp. 287-328, and his book on *Elements of Buddhist Iconography* (Cambridge, Mass.: Harvard University Press, 1935) are very helpful in suggesting some of the ways in which the meaning of the Buddha and his teachings were appropriated and communicated by his early followers. Interesting studies of the early Buddhist doctrine are provided by Edward Conze in his *Buddhist Thought in India* (London: G. Allen and Unwin, 1962) and in Kulatissa N. Jayatilleke's excellent but difficult study of *Early Buddhist Theory of Knowledge* (London: G. Allen and Unwin, 1963). Moreover, concise summaries and critiques of the interpretations developed by the great Buddhologists of earlier generations such as Hermann Oldenberg, Thomas W. Rhys Davids and Caroline Rhys Davids, Th. Stcherbatsky, and Louis La Vallée Poussin are easily accessible in Guy Welbon's impressive study of *The Buddhist Nirvāna and Its Western Interpreters* (Chicago: University of Chicago Press, 1968).

Though the cultic aspect of the tradition has not received the attention which it deserves, a reconstruction of one important ritual is available in Kun Chang, *A Comparative Study of Kathinavastu* ('s Gravenhage: Mouton, 1957), an interesting though far from convincing study of Buddhist initiation rituals which makes reference to the early tradition is contained in Paul Levy, *Buddhism: A Mystery Religion* (London: University of London, 1957), and an important though somewhat technical article has been published by André Bareau on "La Construction et le culte des stupa d'apes les Vinaya Pitakam" in the *Bulletin de l'École Français Extrême-Orient,* L, 2 (1962).[8] For those interested in the communal and social dimensions, the monastic development is discussed in the two volumes of Nalinaksha Dutt's *Early Monastic Buddhism,* 2 vols. (1st ed.; Calcutta: Calcutta Oriental Series, No. 30, 1941) and in Gokuldas De, *Democracy in Buddhist Saṃgha* (Calcutta: Calcutta University Press, 1955) while Asoka and his reign are discussed by Balkrishna Gokhale in *Buddhism and Asoka* (Baroda: Padmaja, 1948), by Fritz Kern in *Asoka: Kaiser und Missionar* (Bern: Francke, 1956) and by Heinz Bechert in "Asoka's 'Schismenedict' und der Begriff Sanghabheda," *Wiener Zeitschrift for die Kunde Sued und Ostaiens,* 5 (1961). (This last item is a more technical study focusing on the relation-

---

[7] A more technical study of many of the sources is contained in André Bareau, *Reserches sur la biographie du Buddha dans les Sūtrapitaka et les Vinayapitaka anciens: de la quête de l'éveil à la conversion de Sariputra et de Maudgalyāyana* (Paris: École Français d'Extrême-Orient, 1963).

[8] The problems involved in the reconstruction and other aspects of the Kathinavastu are further discussed in Heinz Bechert, "Some Remarks on the Kathin Rite," *Journal of the Bihar Society,* LIV, Parts I-V (1968), pp. 319-329.

ships between Asoka and the Buddhist Order). In regard to the Asokan episode, it should also be noted that a translation of the great Emperor's edicts are available in *Edicts of Aśoka*, translated by N. A. Nikam with an introduction by Richard McKeon (Chicago: University of Chicago Press, 1958; in paperbound in Pheonix Books, University of Chicago Press).[9]

If our interests were limited strictly to the development of early Buddhism in India, it would not be appropriate to single out the Theravada strand of the tradition for any special or extraordinary attention. Contrary to the view of many of the philologists who generated the great wealth of scholarship which has been focused on the early Pali texts, the Theravada was only one of a number of sects which developed during the first few centuries of the Buddhist era. (An authoritative discussion of the sectarian development which places the Theravada School in proper perspective is available in André Bareau's *Les sectes bouddhique du Petit Véhicule* (Saigon: École Française d'Extrême-Orient, 1955). However an appreciation of the Theravada orientation is of crucial importance for those who wish to understand the way in which Buddhism developed in Ceylon where the Theravada tradition received its definitive formulation, and where the Theravada Order was ultimately successful in establishing the standards of Buddhist orthodoxy.[10]

Two of the best concise introductions to the Theravada perspective are provided by U Thittila's article on "The Fundamental Principles of Theravada Buddhism" which appears in Kenneth Morgan, ed., *The Path of the Buddha: Buddhism Interpeted by Buddhists* (New York: The Ronald Press, 1956) and in the essay by Isaline Horner (the present President of the Pali Text Society) on "Theravada Buddhism" in R. C. Zaehner, *The Concise Encyclopedia of Living Faiths* (London: Hutchison, 1959), pp. 267-295. Two somewhat lengthier works which can also be utilized at the introductory level are Walpola Rahula's *What the Buddha Taught* (New York: Grove Press, 1962) and George Allen's *The Buddha's Philosophy; Selections from the Pali Canon and an Introductory Essay* (New York: Macmillan, 1959). Moreover, Hermann Oldenberg's study of *Buddha: His Life, His Doctrine, His Order* (London: Williams and Norgate,

---

[9] Those who intend to explore specific subjects which begin with the letters A-Bh (Bharhut) should also consult Gunapala Malalasekera, ed., *Encyclopedia of Buddhism* (Vol. I and supplement, and Vol. II, fasc. 1-4; Colombo: Government of Ceylon, 1961-   ). Additional sections will appear as they are completed. This applies not only to subjects within the area of early Buddhism, but also to subjects related to the Theravada and Sinhalese traditions as well.

[10] In the discussion which follows we have limited the scope of our references by focusing our attention on books, articles, and translations which relate primarily to the canonical, semi-canonical, and early scholastic aspects of the Theravada tradition. Other items which need to be consulted in order to develop an understanding of the Theravada as a full fledged living religion are included in the final section of our essay which deals with Sinhalese Buddhism. Those who are interested in studies which discuss Theravada developments in Southeast Asia should consult the appropriate sections of the bibliography on "Buddhism" by Richard Gard which appears in Charles Adams, ed., *A Reader's Guide to the Great Religions* (New York and London: Free Press and Collier-Macmillan, 1965).

1882, reprinted 1928) is a masterpiece which, despite its acceptance of many
of the mistaken assumptions of the late 19th century intellectual environment in
which it was produced, can still be read with considerable profit.

For those who wish to explore more specific aspects of the tradition there
are a variety of materials available. In the area of conceptual structure and development Donald Swearer has written an interesting doctoral dissertation entitled "Knowledge as Salvation: A Study of Early Buddhism" (unpublished
Ph.D. dissertation, Princeton University, 1965; available at University Micro-
films, Ann Arbor, Michigan), and J. Kashyap has published a two volume work
on *The Abhidhamma Philosophy: The Psycho-Ethical Philosophy of Early Buddhism* (Sarnath: The Mahabodhi Society, 1942, 1943), and R. Spence Hardy
has included the important cosmological and cosmogonic aspects of the tradition
in the early chapters of his *A Manual of Buddhism* (London: Williams and
Norgate, 1880). Isaline Horner has discussed the crucial subject of the early
Theravada ideal in *The Early Buddhist Theory of Man Perfected: A Study of
the Arhat* (London: Williams and Norgate, 1936), while a basic Theravada
meditation text has been translated and discussed by Bhikkhu Nyanaponika in
his *Heart of Buddhist Meditation (Satipatthāna): A Handbook of Mental Training Based on the Buddha's Way of Mindfulness, with an Anthology of Relevant
Texts from the Pali* (New York: Citadel Press, 1969).[11] Two highly significant,
but generally neglected subjects have been treated by Isaline Horner in her study
of *Women under Primitive Buddhism: Laywomen and Almswomen* (New York:
E. P. Dutton and Company, Ltd., 1930) and by Joseph Masson in his examination of *La religion populaire dans le Canon Bouddhique Pali* (Louvain: Bureaux
du Museon, 1942). In addition, the political and historical dimensions are analyzed by Balkrishna Gokhale in his article on "The Early Buddhist View of the
State," *Journal of the American Oriental Society*, LXXXIX, 4 (October-Decem-
ber, 1969) and the "Theravada Buddhist View of History," *Journal of the
American Oriental Society*, 85, 3 (July-September, 1965).[12]

The same interest in the Theravada tradition which has stimulated the production of a great number of interpretive studies has also led scholars to make
available many of the primary sources. General surveys of this primary material
are available in Wilhelm Geiger, *Pali Literature and Language* (Calcutta: University of Calcutta, 1953), and in the two volumes of Bimala Churn Law, *A
History of Pali Literature* (London: Kegan Paul, Trench, Trubner and Co., Ltd.,
1933) while the Sinhalese recollections have been considered in Gunapala Malalasekera, *The Pali Literature of Ceylon* (London: Royal Asiatic Society, 1928;

[11] Those interested in this subject may also wish to consult the more general study of
Edward Conze on *Buddhist Meditation* (London: G. Allen and Unwin, 1956) and the
discussion of Sinhalese technique in Grace Constant Lounsbery, *Buddhist Meditation in
the Southern School* (London: Kegan Paul, Trench and Trubner, 1950).

[12] For other similar studies by Gokhale see "Early Buddhist Kingship," *Journal of
Asian Studies*, XXVI, 1 (November, 1966), pp. 15-22 and "Dhammiko Dhammaraja: A
Study in Buddhist Constitutional Concepts," *Indica*, the Indian Historical Research Insti-
tute Silver Jubilee Commemoration Volume (Bombay, 1963).

reprinted; Colombo: M. D. Gunasena and Co., 1958). Moreover, different types of study aids have been provided by Isaline Horner's revised version of Arthur March, "An Analysis of the Pali Canon" which appears in Christmas Humphreys, ed., *A Buddhist Student's Manual* (London: The Buddhist Society, 1956), by Bhikkhu Nyantiloka in his *Guide through the Abhidhamma Pitaka* (Colombo: The Associated Newspapers of Ceylon, 1938), and by Gunapala Malalasekera in his very helpful two volume *Dictionary of Pali Names* (London: Pali Text Society, 1960).

Among the many canonical works which have been translated into English *Woven Cadences* (tr. by E. M. Hare and issued in a second edition by the Pali Text Society [hereafter PTS] as item No. 15[18] in its Sacred Books of the Buddhists Series [hereafter SBB], 1948), the *Psalms of the Sisters* (presently the only available translation is one by Caroline Rhys Davids which was issued by the PTS as item No. 1* in its Translation Series ([hereafter TrS] in 1909 and reprinted in 1964; however a new English version by K. R. Norman is now in press and will soon be released by PTS as No. 40 in the TrS under the title, *The Elder's Verses*, Vol. II), and the *Dhammapada* (among the many translations the one which best combines accuracy with something of the literary grace of the original is that of P. Lal which is available in paperback [New York: Farrar Straus and Giroux, 1967; in paperback from Noonday Press]), are especially useful in conveying the flavor of the early Theravada piety. *Woven Cadences* is generally recognized as one of the most archaic segments of the canon; the *Psalms of the Sisters* is an inspiring collection of poems attributed to the early Buddhist nuns; and the *Dhammapada* is a text which has often been considered to be the most appealing work produced by the entire tradition. In addition those who wish to press further may consult Isaline Horner, tr., *The Book of the Discipline* (SBB; nos. 10*, 11*, 13*, 14*, 20*, 25*; 1938-1966), Thomas W. and Caroline Rhys Davids, tr., *Dialogues of the Buddha* (SBB, Nos. 2*, 3*, 4*, 1899-1921), Isaline Horner, tr., *The Middle Length Sayings* (TrS; Nos. 29*, 30*, 31*; 1954-1959); Caroline Rhys Davids and F. L. Woodward, tr., *The Book of Kindred Sayings* (TrS; Nos. 7*, 10*, 13*, 14*, 16*; 1917-1930), F. L. Woodward and E. M. Hare, tr., *The Book of Gradual Sayings* (TrS; Nos. 22*, 24*, 25*, 26*, 27; 1932-1936); Bhikkhu Nanamoli, tr., *Minor Readings and Illustrator* (TrS; No. 32*; 1961); F. L. Woodward, B. C. Law, Jean Kennedy, and H. C. Gehman, tr., *Minor Anthologies*, II-IV (SBB; Nos. 8*, 9, 12); Caroline Rhys Davids, *The Buddhist Manual of Psychological Ethics of the Fourth Century being a Translation of the Dhamma-Sangani* (Compendium of States of Phenomenon) (2nd ed.; London: Royal Asiatic Society, 1923); U Thittila, tr., *Book of Analysis* (TrS; No. 39*; 1969); U Narada, tr., *Discourse on Elements* (TrS; No. 34*; 1962); Bimala Churn Law, tr. *A Designation of Human Types* (TrS; No. 12*; 1922); S. Z. Aung and Caroline Rhys Davids, tr., *Points of Controversy* (TrS; No. 5*; 1915); and U Narada, tr., *Conditional Relations Vol. I* (TrS; No. 37*; 1969).

---

[18] Presently in print and available through the Pali Text Society, 62 South Lodge, Circus Road, London, N.W. 8. Asterisks will indicate other items in print.

Though the translation of the semi-canonical texts and commentaries has, of course, proceeded more slowly, there are a number of important works which are now available. Among the immediately post-canonical items one which has exerted a tremendous fascination and appeal is the *Milinda Pañha* which has been translated by Thomas W. Rhys Davids under the title *The Questions of King Milinda* (2 vols.; The Sacred Books of the East, vol. xxx-xxxvi; Oxford: The Clarendon Press, 1890-94; now in Dover paperback) and by Isaline Horner as *Milinda's Questions* (SBB; Nos. 22* and 23*; 1963-64). Other more exegetical texts from the same period which are now available are Bhikkhu Nanamoli, tr., *The Guide* (TrS; No. 33*; 1962), and *Pitaka-Disclosure* (TrS; No. 35*; 1964). Among the later scholastic works the classic is certainly Buddhagosha's *Path of Purity* which has been most adequately translated by Bhikkhu Nanamoli (Colombo, R. Semage, 1960).[14] But in addition to this work which has set the standard for all subsequent Theravada orthodoxy, other scholastically oriented commentaries associated with the great Theravada master are also available. The first to be published was Pe Maung Tin, tr., *The Expositor* (TrS; Nos. 8*, 9*; 1920, 1921, reprinted 1958) which was later followed by Bimala Churn Law, tr., *The Debates Controversy* (on Points of Controversy) (TrS; No. 28*; 1941, reprinted 1969) and N. A. Jayawickrama, tr., *Inception of Discipline* (SBB; No. 21*; 1962). Finally, two other commentaries whose compilation has been attributed to Buddhagosha, and which have had a tremendous impact on popular Buddhism everywhere in the Theravada world, are also available. The first of these is the collection of the accounts of the previous lives of the Buddha which has been published in a multi-volume series edited by E. W. Cowell under the title of *Jataka; or Stories of the Buddha's Former Births* (6 Vols.; Cambridge: University Press, 1895, 1907, 1913 and reprinted in 3 vols., 1969). And the second is the *Dhammapada Commentary* consisting of a collection of tales which recount the occasions when the various stanzas of the *Dhammapada* were spoken; translated by Eugene Burlingame as *Buddhist Legends*, the work was published as Volume XXVIII-XXX in the Harvard Oriental Series (Cambridge, Mass.: Harvard University Press, 1921; reprinted in 3 vols., 1969).

When Buddhism spread from India to Ceylon where it became established in the third century B.C., it entered into a new religious, cultural, and political environment with which it was soon intimately interwoven. In order to gain an appreciation for this environment within which Sinhalese Buddhism took form and has continued to develop for more than two millenia, a number of general historical works may be helpful. A full historical survey which carries up to the mid 1960's is provided by Evelyn F. C. Ludowyk in *A Short History of Ceylon* (2nd ed.; New York: Praeger, 1967)[15] and an overview which em-

---

[14] Though Buddhagosha was not a native of Ceylon his role in the development of Sinhalese Buddhism was very great indeed. For a biographical study see Bimala Churn Law, *The Life and Work of Buddhagosha* (2nd revised ed.; Bombay: Royal Asiatic Society, 1946).

[15] The first and an earlier second edition of the book were published under the title *The Story of Ceylon* by Faber (London), 1962.

phasizes the role of the Sinhalese, Tamil and Moorish communities is available in S. Arasaratnam, *Ceylon* (Englewood Cliffs, N.J.: Prentice Hall, 1964). For the period up to 1500 A.D. a definitive treatment is provided in H. C. Ray, ed., *University of Ceylon, History of Ceylon* (2 parts; Colombo: University of Ceylon, 1959, 1960) which, fortunately, is available in a more usable abridged edition by C. W. Nicholas and Senerat Paranavitana, *A Concise History of Ceylon* (Colombo: University of Ceylon, 1961).[16] Interesting and important studies of the medieval period are available in Wilhelm Geiger, *Culture of Ceylon in Medieval Times*, ed. by Heinz Bechert (Wiesbaden: Otto Harrassowitz, 1960) and in Manikka B. Ariyapala in *Society in Medieval Ceylon: the State of Society in Ceylon as Depicted in the Saddharma-ratnavaliya and other Literature of the Thirteenth Century* (Colombo: K.V.G. de Silva, 1956). Robert Knox provides an extremely observant traveller's account of the situation in the seventeenth century in his *An Historical Relation of the Island Ceylon in the East Indies* (London: Richard Chiswell, printer to The Royal Society which has been published at Rose and Crown, 1681) which has also been published in an abridged edition edited by Evelyn F. C. Ludowyk, *Robert Knox in the Kandayan Kingdom*, (Bombay: Oxford University Press [Indian Branch], 1948); and Ralph Pieris has done a major study on *Sinhalese Social Organization: The Kandyan Period* (Peradeniya: Ceylon University Press Board, 1956). As for the modern era, the most important work is the careful and quite comprehensive study of W. Howard Wriggins called *Ceylon: Dilemmas of a New Nation* (Princeton: Princeton University Press, 1960).

Turning to items which focus more particularly on Buddhism itself, a very basic and concise survey is provided by Charles Eliot in Chapter 35 of the third volume of *Hinduism and Buddhism: An Historical Sketch* (London: Routledge and Kegan Paul, 1954). The most useful and comprehensive account of the earlier tradition is found in Walpola Rahula, *History of Buddhism in Ceylon: The Anuradhapura Period; Third Century B. C.-Tenth Century A. D.* (2nd ed.; Colombo: M. D. Gunasena, 1966), which may be supplemented by E. W. Adikaram's *Early History of Buddhism in Ceylon* (Colombo: Ceylon Daily News Press for D. S. Puswella, 1946), a study which relies primarily on the Pali commentaries of the fifth century A. D. The interested reader may also go directly to the ancient Sinhalese chronicles including Hermann Oldenburg, tr., *The Dipavamsa: An Ancient Buddhist Historical Record* (London: Williams and Norgate, 1879), Wilhelm Geiger assisted by Mabel Brode, tr., *The Mahavamsa or Great Chronicle of Ceylon* (PTS; TrS; No. 3, 1912, and reprinted with an addendum by G. C. Mendis, 1964, and William Geiger assisted by Mabel Rickmers, tr., *The Culavamsa; or the Minor Chronicle of Ceylon* (PTS; TrS; Nos. 18 and 20; 1929, 1930, and reprinted 1969).[17] As for the modern period an excel-

---

[16] The University is still in the process of compiling the second volume which will deal with the more recent centuries.

[17] For corrections to the *Mahavamsa* and *Culavamsa* translations see the appropriate appendices in Geiger, *Culture of Ceylon*.

lent, comprehensive, and thoroughly documented treatment is available in Heinz Bechert, *Buddhismus, Staat und Gesellschaft in den Ländern Theravāda-Buddhismus*, Vol. 1 (Vol. XVII/1 Schriften des Instituts für Asienkunde in Hamburg; Frankfurt and Berlin: Alfred Metzner, 1966).[18] In addition, three important primary sources are available in English. The first of these is a collection of speeches, essays and letters of the great Buddhist leader and reformer of the late nineteenth and early twentieth centuries, Anagarika Dharmapala, edited by Ananda W. P. Guruge and published under the title *Return to Righteousness* (Colombo: Ceylon Government Press, 1965).[19] The second is the abridged English version of the famous Buddhist Committee of Inquiry report, *The Betrayal of Buddhism* (Balangoda: Dharmavijaya Press, 1956) which is a highly polemic recital of the ways in which Buddhism was undermined during the colonial period, and a call for its reestablishment in a preeminent position. The third, and in some ways the most interesting, is D. C. Vijayavardhana's equally polemic *Dharma-Vijaya, Triumph of Righteousness, or The Revolt in the Temple* (Colombo: Sinha Publications, 1953) which was aimed at stimulating both Buddhist reform and the post-independence Buddhist revival.

Though the sectarian and doctrinal aspects of Sinhalese Buddhism have often been treated in rather monolithic terms, there has, in fact, been a great deal of diversity and development over the centuries. The variety of Buddhist traditions which have been represented in the development of Sinhalese Buddhism clearly portrayed in Heinz Bechert, "Zur Geschichte der buddhistischen Sekten in Indien und Ceylon," *Nouvelle Clio*, 7-9 (1955, 1956, 1957), pp. 311-360. In addition to some of the previously cited works which deal with the predominant Theravada tradition the reader should also consult works which discuss the role of other sects such as Senerat Paranavitana's important article on "Mahayanism in Ceylon," *Ceylon Journal of Science*, Section G, II, 1 (December 1928), pp. 37-51, Martin Wickramasinghe, "Tantrism in Ceylon and Tisa Veva Lithic Diagram," *Ceylon Historical Journal* (Dehivela), I, 4 (April, 1952), pp. 287-292, and R. A. H. L. Gunawardana, "Buddhist Nikayas in Medieval Ceylon," *Ceylon Journal of Historical and Social Studies* (Peradeniya), IX, (1966), pp. 55-66. And beyond this it is essential to take into account the way in which the classical Theravada beliefs and ideals have gradually been adapted to changing conditions and new problematics. In this connection a number of interesting studies are available including Gananath Obeyesekere's article on "Theodicy, Sin and Salvation in a Sociology of Buddhism" in Edmund Leach, ed., *Dialectic in Practical Religion* (Cambridge Papers in Social Anthropology, No. 5; Cambridge: Cam-

---

[18] Volume II deals with the modern Theravada developments in Burma, Cambodia, and Laos, with an excursus on Vietnam. Volume III, which is not yet published, will provide a comprehensive bibliography which should prove to be an invaluable aid to further research.

[19] According to Heinz Bechert this work is marred by the fact that the editor has made arbitrary changes in the text which will be specifically noted by W. Halbfass in his chapter on "Anagarika Dharmapala" in *Das Christentum im Urteil seiner Gegner*, ed. by K. Deschner, forthcoming.

bridge University, 1968), Richard Gombrich, "Merit Transference in Sinhalese Buddhism: Case Study of the Interaction between Doctrine and Practice," *History of Religions Journal*, Vol. XI, 2 (November, 1971), pp. 203-219; and Marguerite Robinson " 'The House of the Mighty Hero' or 'The House of Enough Paddy': Some Implications of a Sinhalese Myth" in Leach, ed., *Dialectic in Practical Religion*.[20]

The way in which Theravada Buddhism has been appropriated in Ceylon has been further analyzed in a variety of other anthropological works which deal more specifically with the relationships which it has developed with Hindu and local religious traditions. Among these the most interesting studies are perhaps Michael Ames, "Magical Animism and Buddhism: A Structural Analysis of the Sinhalese Religious System" in Edward Harper, ed., *Religion in South Asia* (Seattle: University of Washington, 1964), and Gananath Obeyesekere, "The Buddhist Pantheon and Its Extensions" in Manning Nash, ed., *Anthropological Studies of Theravada Buddhism* (New Haven: Yale University Press, 1968). Those who are interested in the kinds of problems dealt with in these discussions may also wish to consult Gananath Obeyesekere, "The Great Tradition and the Little Tradition in the Perspective of Sinhalese Buddhism," *Journal of Asian Studies*, XXII, 2 (February, 1963), pp. 139-153; Michael Ames, "Ritual Presentations and the Structure of the Sinhalese Pantheon," in Nash, ed., *Anthropological Studies*; Michael Ames, "Buddha and Dancing Goblins: A Theory of Magic and Religion," *American Anthropologist*, LXVI, 1 (February, 1964), pp. 75-82; Hans-Dieter Evers, "Buddha and the Seven Gods: The Dual Organization of a Temple in Central Ceylon," *Journal of Asian Studies*, XXVII, 3, pp. 541-550; Edmund Leach, "Pulleyer and the Lord Buddha: An Aspect of Religious Syncretism in Ceylon," *Psychoanalysis and the Psychoanalytic Review*, XLIX, 2 (1962), pp. 80-102; and Richard Gombrich, "Food for Seven Grandmothers," *Man*, VI, 1 (March, 1971), pp. 5-17.[21]

In order to gain a balanced understanding of Sinhalese Buddhism it is necessary to give serious attention not only to the doctrinal aspects as such, but also to the traditions of Buddhist art, symbolism, and the cultic life with which they have been very closely correlated. A comprehensive study which deals with the

[20] From the title and the author's references in his already published writing it is clear that Richard Gombrich's *Precept and Practice: Traditional Buddhism in the Rural Highlands of Ceylon* (Oxford: Clarendon Press, 1971) deals with this topic in detail.

[21] Similar kinds of studies have been done in other Theravada countries. For Burma see Melford Spiro, *Burmese Supernaturalism: A Study of the Explanation and Reduction of Suffering* (Englewood Cliffs, N. J.: Prentice-Hall, 1967) and *Buddhism and Society; A Great Tradition and Its Burmese Vicissitudes* (New York: Harper and Row, 1970). For Thailand see S. J. Tambiah, *Buddhism and Spiritual Cults in Northeastern Thailand* (Cambridge, Eng.: University Press, 1970). For Laos see Frank Reynolds, "Ritual and Social Hierarchy: An Aspect of Traditional Religion in Buddhist Laos," *History of Religions Journal*, IX, 1 (August, 1969), pp. 78-79. For some comparative observations see Heinz Bechert, "Eine Fragen der Religionssoziologie und Stocktur der suedasiatischen Buddhismus," *International Yearbook for the Sociology of Religion*, IV (1969), pp. 251-295.

artistic tradition at both the classical and folk levels is Ananada Coomaraswamy's *Medieval Sinhalese Art: Being a Monograph on Medieval Sinhalese Arts and Crafts Mainly as Surviving in the Eighteenth Century with an Account of the Structure of Society and the Station of the Craftsmen,* (2nd edition; New York: Pantheon Books with the Patronage of the Ceylon Government, 1956), while many aspects of Buddhist symbolism and cult in Ceylon are brilliantly interpreted by Paul Mus in *Barabadur, passim.* However the general reader will find much more focused and accessible treatments in Evelyn F. C. Ludowyk's examination of the architectural and artistic heritage in *The Footprint of the Buddha* (London: Allen and Unwin, 1958) and Senerat Paranavitana's essay on "Buddhist Festivals in Ceylon" in B. C. Law, ed., *Buddhistic Studies* (Calcutta and Simla: Thacker Spink, 1931). Buddhist iconography is discussed in D. T. Devandra, *The Buddhist Image and Ceylon* (Colombo: K. V. G. de Silva and Sons, 1957) while a related cultic practice is described by Richard Gombrich in his article on "The Consecration of a Buddha Image," *Journal of Asian Studies,* XXVI, 1 (November, 1966), pp. 23-26. Senerat Paranavitana has contributed an important monograph on *The Stupa in Ceylon* (Colombo: Ceylon Government, 1946) which can be profitably supplemented by a study of the *Thupavamsa or Chronicle of the Stupa* (a new translation by N. A. Jayawickrama is being published by the PTS and should be available before the end of 1972) which is devoted largely to the construction of the Maha Stupa by King Dutthagamani, and by comments on the political significance of the stupa cult by Paul Mus in his introductory article in René Berval, ed., *Présence du Bouddhisme* (Saigon: France-Asie, 1959) which is entitled "Bouddhisme et monde occidental; pour une nouvelle methode." Though there is as yet no comprehensive treatment of the cult of the relics, two important studies deal with the traditions associated with the Tooth Relic, which became the palladium of the Sinhalese nation; the first is Arthur M. Hocart, *The Temple of the Tooth in Kandy* (Memoirs of the Archaeological Survey of Ceylon, Vol. IV; London: Luzac, for the government of Ceylon, 1931), while the second, which consciously seeks to supplement Hocart's study, is Victor Goloubew, "La Temple de la Dent à Kandy," *Bulletin de L'École Français Extrême-Orient,* XXXII (1932), pp. 441-474. The cult of the Buddha's Footprint is taken into account by Senerat Paranavitana in his study of *The God of Adam's Peak* (Ascona: Artibus Asiae, 1957). And finally, the extremely important Paritta ceremonies (these are ceremonies which utilize the recitation of special portions of the sacred scriptures as a means to drive away evil influences are discussed in different ways by Otaker Pertold, "A Protective Ritual of the Southern Buddhists," *Journal of the Anthropological Society of Bombay,* XII, 6 (1923), pp. 744-789, by Ernst Waldschmidt in his *Von Ceylon bis Turfan. Schriften für Geschichte, Literatur, Religion und Kunst des indischen Kulturraumes* (Göttingen: Vandenhoech and Ruprecht, 1967), pp. 456-478, and by Nur Yalman in a very interesting anthropological study entitled "The Structure of Sinhalese Healing Rituals" which appears in Edward Harper, ed., *Religion in South Asia.*

At the level of communal order and development a number of specific studies are also available. Heinz Bechert has provided a discussion of the early connection between Buddhism and Sinhalese nationalism in his "Uber den Ursprung der Geschichtsschreibund im indischen Kulturbereich" which was published in *Nachrichen der Akademie der Wissenschaften in Goettingen, Philologisch-historische Klasse*, 1969, 2, pp. 35-58, and an excellent survey in "Theravada Buddhist Samgha: Some General Observations on Historical and Political Factors in its Development," *Journal of Asian Studies*, XXIX, 4 (August, 1970), pp. 761-778.[22] Interesting studies of the relationships between the Sinhalese Sangha and other parts of the Buddhist world are found in W. Pachow, "Ancient Cultural Relations between Ceylon and China," *University of Ceylon Review*, XII, 3 (July, 1954), pp. 182-191; in Senerat Paranavitana, "The Religious Intercourse between Ceylon and Siam in the Thirteenth and Fifteenth Centuries," *Journal of the Royal Asiatic Society, Ceylon Branch*, XXXII, 85 (1932), pp. 190-212; and P. E. E. Fernando, "An Account of the Kandyan Mission sent to Siam in 1750 A. D.," *Ceylon Journal of Historical and Social Studies* (Peradeniya), II, 1 (January, 1959), pp. 37-83. The contemporary Buddhist Order is surveyed by André Bareau, *La vie et l'organisation des communautés Bouddhiques modernes de Ceylon* (Pondicherry: Institut Français d'Indologie, 1957), while Hans-Dieter Evers treats the very important but often neglected economic involvement of the Order and its members in his article on "Monastic Landlordism in Ceylon," *Journal of Asian Studies*, XXVIII, 4 (August, 1969), pp. 685-692 and "Kinship and Property Rights in a Buddhist Monastery in Central Ceylon," *American Anthropologist*, LXIX, 6 (December, 1967), pp. 703-710.

Alongside these works there are also a number of items which deal more specifically with the problems encountered by the Buddhist community during the period of British occupation, and with the nineteenth and twentieth century struggle for reform and renewal. Various aspects of the colonial period are considered by Hans-Dieter Evers in "Buddhism and British Colonial Policy in Ceylon: 1815-1875," *Asian Studies* (University of the Philippines, Queyzon City), II, 3 (December, 1964), pp. 323-333 and by K. M. de Silva in "Buddhism and the British Government in Ceylon," *Ceylon Historical Journal* (Dehiwela) X, 1-4 (July 1960-April, 1961), pp. 91-160. And different dimensions of the struggle for religious revival and national development are discussed by Bardwell Smith in "Toward a Buddhist Anthropology: The Problems of the Secular," *Journal of the American Academy of Religion*, XXXVI, 3 (September, 1968), pp. 203-216; by Donald K. Swearer in "Lay Buddhism and the Buddhist Revival in Ceylon," *Journal of the American Academy of Religion*, XXXVIII, 3 (September, 1970), pp. 255-275; by Michael Ames in "Ideological and Social Change in Ceylon," Human Organization, XXII, 1 (Spring, 1963), pp. 45-53; by Ames again in his "Religion, Politics, and Economic Development in Ceylon: an Interpretation of the Weber Thesis" published in Melford Spiro, ed., *Symposium on*

---

[22] Though Bechert's discussion is not limited to Ceylon, the greater part of his discussion is devoted to the development of the Sinhalese tradition.

New Approaches to the Study of Religion (Proceedings of the Annual Spring Meeting of the American Ethnological Society; Seattle: University of Washington, 1964); by C. D. S. Siriwardene in "Buddhist Reorganization in Ceylon" published in Donald E. Smith, ed., *South Asian Politics and Religion* (Princeton: Princeton University Press, 1966); by Ediriweera R. Sarachandra in "Traditional Values and the Modernization of a Buddhist Society: The Case of Ceylon" published in Robert Bellah, ed., *Religion and Progress in Modern Asia* (New York and London: Free Press and Macmillan, 1965); and by Hans-Dieter Evers in "Buddhistische Gesellsachaftsordnung und Buddhistischer Wohlfahrtsstaat— Religionssoziologische Grundlagen des Ceylonischen Nationalismus," *Modern Welt, Zeitschrift für vergleichend Geistesgeschichtliche Soziolwissenschaftlich Forschung*, IV, 3 (1963), pp. 265-277.[23] For more normative approaches the reader may wish to consult O. H. de A. Wijesekera, *Buddhism and Society* (Colombo: M. D. Gunasena, 1951), Gunapala Malalasekera, *Buddhism and the Race Question* (Paris: UNESCO, 1958); and J. R. Jayewardene, *Buddhism, Marxism, and Other Essays* (London: East and West, 1957). In order to gain some insight into the importance and meaning of the religio-political celebrations which were held in 1956 to commemorate the 2500th anniversary of the Buddha's entrance into his Parinibbana, and the supposedly simultaneous establishment of the Sinhalese race, the Buddhist Council of Ceylon, ed., *An Event of Dual Significance* (Colombo: Lanka Bauddha Mandalya, 1956) may be consulted.[24] And for an insight into a very different and often neglected aspect of the thrust toward Buddhist reform and revival in the 1950's see Nur Yalman, "The Ascetic Buddhist Monks of Ceylon," *Ethnology*, I, 3 (July, 1962), pp. 315-328, reprinted in Peter Hammond, ed., *Cultural and Social Anthropology: Selected Readings* (New York: Macmillan, 1964).[25]

As we have proceeded in our essay from the section on early Buddhism to the section dealing with the Theravada School, to the section focused on Sinhalese Buddhism, our selections have become increasingly numerous. However it is still true that even in the final discussion of the Sinhalese tradition we have only touched the surface of the available materials. For those who may wish to press further, other references relevant to each of the areas which we have covered, ref-

---

[23] Those interested in parallel developments in other Theravada countries may consult Donald E. Smith, *Religion and Politics in Burma* (Princeton: Princeton University, 1965) and Emanuel Sarkisyanz, *Buddhist Backgrounds of the Burmese Revolution* (The Hague: Martinus Nijhoff, 1965) as well as the short comparative discussion relating developments in Ceylon and the various Theravada countries in Southeast Asia which is contained in Joseph Kitagawa and Frank Reynolds, "Theravada-Buddhismus im 20. Jahrhundert," published in Heinrich Dumoulin, ed., *Buddhismus der Gegenwart* (Freiburg, et al.: Herder, 1970.

[24] A discussion of the traditional background revelant to the importance of the 2500 year anniversary is contained in George Coedes', "The Twenty-Five-Hundredth Anniversary of the Buddha," *Diogenes*, XV (July, 1956), pp. 95-111.

[25] Those interested in comparing the situation in Ceylon with that which developed in Burma may wish to consult Winston King, *In Hope of Nirvana: An Essay on Theravada Buddhist Ethics* (LaSalle, Illinois: Open Court, 1964).

erences to numerous works dealing with other aspects of Buddhism, and references to important research tools and periodicals are all contained in Richard Gard's chapter on "Buddhism" in Charles Adams, ed., *A Reader's Guide to the Great Religions* (New York and London: Free Press and Macmillan, 1965). And for those who wish to go still further and undertake a serious study of a particular problem, excellent research bibliographies are available for both Buddhism and Ceylon. The most comprehensive source for locating materials on Buddhism is the *Bibliographie Bouddhique* I-XXXII and continuing (Librarie Orientaliste; Paris: Paul Geuthner, 1930-1967) while the literature on Ceylon, including Sinhalese Buddhism, has been comprehensively surveyed in H. A. I. Goonetileke's excellent *Bibliography of Ceylon* (2 Vol. Bibliotheca Asiatica 5; Zug, Switzerland: Inter Documentation Company, 1970). Finally, the annual bibliographical issue of the *Journal of Asian Studies* provides both the general reader and the specialist with a useful and accessible means for keeping up to date on some of the major publications concerning Buddhism, and most of the important literature which deals with Ceylon.